True Hospitality

True Hospitality

*Lessons Learned
from Behind
the Concierge Desk*

Jamie Cooperstein

GFB

Published by GFB™, Seattle
www.girlfridayproductions.com

Produced by Girl Friday Productions

Cover design: Emily Weigel
Developmental editor: Matthew Patin
Production editorial: Reshma Kooner
Project management: Kim Kent

Image credits: cover © Shutterstock/ Lapina, Shutterstock/Karen Culp

ISBN (paperback): 978-1-964721-32-3
ISBN (ebook): 978-1-964721-33-0

Library of Congress Control Number 2024921607

First edition

To uniformed hourly workers past, present, and future.

You stand on unforgiving floors,
you work on weekends and holidays,
you are underpaid,

and you still selflessly put others' needs before your own.

Thank you for your service!

CONTENTS

Prologue xi

Pre-Arrival 1

Arrival 13

Occupancy 85

Departure 145

Post-Stay 149

Acknowledgments 155

Discussion Guide 159

About the Author 163

PROLOGUE

In the foyer, I kiss my six-year-old daughter, Josephine, and say goodbye.

"Mommy has teaching today," I say. "I'm off to talk about pineapples. Only two sleeps." I've taught her that a pineapple is the symbol of hospitality, and I help others to make fabulous first impressions.

I reach down and hug her, and she latches on tight.

Later, as I fly to a conference in Florida to deliver a keynote on the customer experience, I contemplate how I got here.

When one door seemingly closed, another unexpectedly opened, and the wonderful world of hospitality and the joy of serving others found me at the perfect time. I never expected that putting on a concierge uniform would lead me to my calling.

This is my story.

PRE-ARRIVAL

TWISTS AND TURNS

I was fourteen, wide-eyed in the den of my childhood home watching acclaimed US gymnast Kerri Strug. She ran to the vault, springboarded herself, flipped through the air, and fell. She was hurt and limping badly.

She couldn't possibly complete her second vault, could she?

Yet she lined up again. I saw the determination on her face and the focus in her eyes. She sprinted, hit the springboard, and landed on one foot. She threw her arms overhead. Moments later, the judges announced she'd won it for the Magnificent Seven at the 1996 Olympic summer games in Atlanta, Georgia. I threw my arms up as well.

Later in the telecast, Bob Costas, the NBC sports broadcaster and primetime anchor for the Olympics, interviewed Kerri Strug, and I moved closer to the TV, enamored by how effortlessly he asked about her injury, the iconic vault, and team gold. The two of them bantered like old friends. I wanted to be like that—like Bob. It hit me. That's what I want to do! I want to be the one asking questions, interviewing Kerri with her foot bandaged and a gold medal around her neck. I thought, *How do I get a microphone in my hand?*

Four months later I became the announcer for my high school's swimming and diving team. I wanted to work on my broadcaster voice. I sat behind a folding table on the pool deck wearing a turtleneck, corduroys, and my favorite Doc Martens, overheating and fighting frizz at every home meet. I was given a microphone to announce the judges scores and shown how to turn it on. I figured out the rest.

I flicked the switch. "Up next, Jason Coben, doing a forward one-and-a-half somersault with a twist. . . ."

"The scores are . . . 8.5, 9, and 9.5."

The home crowd cheered. I felt terrified. It wasn't easy pretending to be confident, but I loved being in control. I also loved to write, and maybe I could be a broadcaster who wrote their own script. But I needed to learn the craft.

I asked my favorite English teacher and newspaper adviser, Thom Williams, for pointers on journalistic writing.

"Go with what you got there," he said, and lead with the who, what, when, where, and why.

By senior year I had my own column: Coop's Quotes, which highlighted ten quotes. My favorite was from Ralph Waldo Emerson: "Do not go where the path may lead; go instead where there is no path and leave a trail."

I was inspired to forge a path very few women took.

In my freshman year of college, I wrote game recaps for the student newspaper. I sat in the stands for a women's soccer match (oy, soccer games are long), interviewed the coach postgame, and wrote up the story before nine that night. The next day I saw my byline and smiled. I saved my press clippings for my portfolio in a three-ring binder.

Sophomore year I secured the job as anchor for our

on-campus news station. I wore a collared blouse on air and read scripts. I reported on the new Mexican station in the dining hall and the conflicts of Greek life on campus. I saved all the VHS footage to make a professional reel.

Junior year I became a part-time sportswriter at *The Trenton Times*, a daily newspaper. Out of a group of about fifteen, most were men my dad's age, and I was the only woman. When Jed, the senior copyeditor, invited me to his fantasy football draft at his home in Yardley, I knew I not only belonged but was also accepted.

Senior year I interned with the Philadelphia 76ers in the PR department, recording postgame interviews and distributing quotes to the local media. I ate pregame dinners with men like Howard Eskin, known for his on-air banter, wearing a long movie-star fur coat, and pissing off team owners; and John Smallwood, the friendly beat writer for the *Philadelphia Daily News*, who wore oversize polo shirts and loose pants. I was as excited to be around the conversation of the reporting as I was to be around NBA all-star Allen Iverson.

I found encouragement on each rung of the ladder. "Great job, Jamie," Mom would say. "You're going to make it someday." My professors would compliment me on my diction, and I felt validated when my internship supervisor said, "I can see your passion, Jamie."

I agreed.

My final internship before college graduation seemed like a formality. I would soon be moving someplace like Topeka or Bismarck—entry-level markets for an aspiring broadcaster. I imagined I'd make $12,000 a year and work weekends covering the local rodeo or county fair. Even Bob Costas had to start somewhere, I'd remind myself.

The spring of senior year, 2003, I stood in the Fox 29 newsroom hiding my armpit sweat, waiting with great anticipation as Paul, my mentor, a tall and lanky sports producer, stood with his arms crossed and reviewed my three-minute demo tape. I paced around that dingy windowless room in the back of the station, nervously ironed out the creases in my blue cotton blouse, and waited for him to speak, to turn around and say, "You're incredible. You have a future in front of the camera! Send it out today."

And why wouldn't he? I'd teed everything up, after all: made fifty duplicates of my demo tape, bought bubble mailers, researched the addresses for small stations nationwide.

But with his eyes focused on the screen ahead, Paul eventually said what I did *not* want to hear: "You're too local."

My first instinct was to say, "Wait! You didn't see me with my blazer. And the story about the lacrosse team!" But I just held my stomach, queasy. His three words— "You're too local"—replayed over and over.

"Oh, really?" I said, fighting back tears.

"Yeah. I don't want to see you waste your time halfway across the country to never make it back east in front of a camera. Consider a different path. One as a writer or producer, like me."

He pressed the eject button and handed me back my tape. I took it with me to the bathroom. This was the only path I'd known since age fourteen. Never did I imagine that my upbringing in Delaware County, Pennsylvania— or Delco, where water was referred to as *wooder*—would have professional implications.

—

I continued my internship learning TV production two days a week. I logged game footage to be edited for B-roll and went out on shoots with cameramen. I stared at game footage for hours on end, recording time and date stamps on the highlights. These short snippets of three-pointers and home runs would then be spliced together and played while Don Tollefson, the main anchor, was talking so the viewer wasn't just staring at his head. For a sports fanatic, it was fun, but I still longed to be in front of the camera.

A week later, determined, I sent out those fifty mailers with demo tapes to see what would happen. Nobody called.

About a month after my job-application marathon, still with no luck, I got a job as a tour guide at the Wells Fargo Center, the home of the 76ers and Flyers. I craved to hear friends and family say, "You're on the right track," and listen to the oohs and aahs. But what I didn't say was that I walked backward most days.

I recounted with the tourists the history of our basketball and hockey teams and shared fun facts, such as how it took two hours and ten minutes to change the floor from an ice rink to a basketball court. I gestured to the retired shirts in the rafters and to the banner indicating the number of Billy Joel sellouts. In the locker room, megafans touched hangers that held their idols' jerseys and sat on benches where star players tied their shoes or skates. I loved going off script, too, and encouraged casual banter among the crowd: Where are you from? How old are your kids? Who is your favorite player?

Two months later I became an account manager, selling season tickets in a windowless room beside the Zamboni parking. My mission was simple: Call up every single-game ticket purchaser from the past five years and entice them to buy a season ticket package. Most calls ended with a swift no.

As the holidays approached, I was assigned to sell "Santa Sacks" (two tickets, hot dogs, drinks, and an auto-graphed puck) at a kiosk at the King of Prussia mall. Five days a week, I sat across from the Coach store, waving to shoppers and trying to sell holiday gift packages, praying the Flyers logo was enough to lure them.

Meanwhile, I admired the Israeli Dead Sea salesman who worked the kiosk next to mine. "Ladies! Ladies!" he'd bark. "Have you considered some Dead Sea mud to take ten years off your life? Right this way!" Then he'd put his arm around them and usher them to the kiosk.

I need to be more like him, I thought. My new line be-came "Have you been to a Flyers game this year? No? Let me tell you about what we have coming up!"

What I learned was nobody goes to the mall to buy from a kiosk. In April, rumors of a lockout circulated, and no season meant no job. So I returned to Fox 29, this time with an eye on being a writer and producer.

As a production assistant for the 10:00 p.m. news, I chased blood. If it bleeds, it leads, the saying goes. Everything else became yesterday's news. I sat in the newsroom, waiting for the police scanners—fires, crashes, murders, shootings. I played the go-between, the per-son scanning the 911 police dispatch and scheduling the cameraman and reporter. I also controlled the speed of the teleprompter, a flashlight-size roll that moved text for

Dawn Stensland, our veteran anchor. I didn't breathe for thirty minutes at a time.

After three months, feeling full of doom and gloom and anxiety, I called my mom one night while I was driving home. "I hate this," I said. I had to get out of there.

"Speak with Cousin Jeffrey," she said, aware that a 9-to-5 desk job wouldn't suit me.

Yes, I had a bit of the ADD thing going on, and keeping busy in a high-energy environment, like the hotel where Jeffrey worked in HR, might be perfect. I knew the Rittenhouse was fancy, though I had never been inside. But would it be like the expensive store in the mall where you don't feel comfortable entering in your street clothes? Or like the prestigious Aronimink Golf Club, where my college boyfriend was a legacy member and I was forced to wear tennis whites? Both were like entering a walk-in freezer.

The wealth at the Rittenhouse could be intimidating, but maybe working, rather than simply *being*, in a highbrow setting would be more comfortable? I had always felt a greater connection with Aronimink's hourly staff, who shared with me a similar upbringing. I figured a lot of young people worked at the Rittenhouse as well, and over the years Jeffrey had spoken of the privilege of creating a home away from home for celebrities, politicians, musicians, professional athletes, and international travelers.

Whatever the case, I was so eager for a change I would have said yes to working the coat check, so I thanked my mom for the suggestion, took her advice, and soon gave my cousin a call.

Jeffrey promised only an interview with the frontoffice manager, Lucia. So come the day of the interview, wearing my only suit—a classic navy blue pinstripe—and my kitten heels, I took a deep breath and walked up the circular driveway to the Rittenhouse's front entrance.

A uniformed doorman opened the ornate brass door and escorted me to the reception area, the sound of clacking footsteps filling the space. I was nervous, both because of the luxurious environment I found myself in and because this would be my only chance to secure a role at a prestigious hotel. While I waited, I looked around and saw marble everywhere—the floor, the pillars, the walls. One of those pillars sported a fancy-looking award plaque indicating something called AAA Five Diamond status.

"Good afternoon, Jamie," said a woman in her early forties dressed in a dark suit and flats. She introduced herself as Lucia. "Welcome. Right this way." She gestured to a table in a lounge adjacent to a room marked the Mary Cassatt Tea Room. Together we passed a circular table with a fresh flower arrangement unlike any I'd seen before—higher than my head and so thick with blooms that I couldn't see through it.

Lucia must have noticed my astonishment. "It's changed out weekly," she said, "by the on-site florist."

When I was growing up, my family stayed at budget hotels for my softball tournaments. The kinds of places that had Bibles in nightstand drawers much more often than giant, unmissable fresh bouquets in lobbies. Not until I watched *Home Alone 2* and *Pretty Woman*, with their legendary hotels and crisply dressed, smiling staff, did I understand that not all hotels were created equal. In the movies, the employees' uniforms gave them a voice and power, and the entire guest experience—good or bad— seemed to rest on their shoulders.

Once Lucia and I reached the lounge, I sank into a chair and felt proud to be interviewing and confident that I'd get the front desk job. All I had to do was smile and give out room keys, right? Who can't do that?

Not so fast. The front desk associate was responsible for balancing a bank of money during each shift, Lucia told me. I would be documenting every guest transaction. What's more, guests often came to the front desk to exchange foreign currencies, which meant I had to memorize daily rates.

Flashbacks from seventh-grade algebra hit me, and my eyes must have been wide because Lucia, likely detecting my fear, broke the silence.

"Well?" she said flatly. "Why are you here?"

I panicked—would she think my uneasiness meant a bad fit for the job? But I took a deep breath. "I am a proud Philadelphian," I said. "I want to showcase our city's positive aspects, which are often overlooked in the local news coverage. I want to help guests have a wonderful stay!"

She must have sensed my passion, because I was offered a position on the spot, as a concierge for $10.50 an hour.

"You start next week," she said.

And just like that, a rabbit was pulled out of a hat.

I had never ever thought of being a concierge. Never. I knew what a concierge was only because my family had stayed in a nice hotel in New York City for my eighteenth birthday and my parents had engaged one for a pretheater dinner recommendation. My dad said thank you by placing a five-dollar bill in their hand.

Would that now be me? Would I have the expertise necessary to warrant a tip?

I had no idea how a twenty-two-year-old from nearby Delco, a mostly blue-collar area, was to be a Five Diamond concierge. I still lived at my parents' home, and my favorite place to meet my friends was Ruby Tuesday. I had no experience. No contacts. No firsthand recommendations. *Five Diamond* occupied a tall pedestal in my mind, and I had to figure out how to climb it while hiding my insecurities.

As I drove home, I called my mom. "You aren't going to believe it!"

Little did I know this would become the start of a new career.

ARRIVAL

REPORTING FOR DUTY

On my first day at the Rittenhouse in May 2004, I was told to use the back entrance. I arrived early and couldn't wait to get my uniform. I perked up as if I were a Broadway actor reporting to work via the stage door. At the back of the hotel, I found a banged-up aluminum door with a small inconspicuous sign that read Employee Entrance. It slammed behind me.

Inside I met Estelle, the stocky purchasing director, who tracked down anything and everything for the hotel, from holiday turkeys to soap. The smell of a fish delivery caught my attention, as did her locked cages filled with supplies. I came to learn that Estelle always had a large stash of boxes in front of her—meat for the restaurant, computer paper for the executive office, or robes for the spa. Her job was to distribute these purchases around the hotel without a guest ever seeing their path of travel.

Next to her was the security command post, with access to records of every key swipe made by employees or guests and video footage of every square inch of the hotel except behind guest room doors. The security team, a mix of ex-military and brawny former standout athletes, was also responsible for making sure employees didn't take anything home that didn't belong to them. I became chummy with the guys in this department, as they managed the lost and found and it became my job to generate shipping labels for items left behind.

The back of house reminded me of a New York City subway. The lobby's shiny marble surfaces felt like they belonged in an entirely different zip code. I wasn't allowed to clock in until I was in uniform, so I followed the fish-smelling cinder block hallway to the laundry department and hauled my heavy uniform pieces to the shared ladies' locker room. The fantasy of my "costume" waiting for me in a private dressing room with a team of stylists would have to be reserved for my debut alongside dream-costar Hugh Jackman.

I sat down on the cold wooden bench and fiddled with the lock I was told to bring. The pale-green lockers brought me back to Marple Newtown Senior High School and changing pre– and post–swim class. My own uniform still had to be fitted and ordered, so in the meantime I put on someone else's old uniform, which felt weird and had a button missing. After dressing, I clocked in and made my way to the lobby, passing through the final door of the employee area that revealed the front-of-house guest spaces.

I smoothed out my uniform and cracked my knuckles.

As I heard my shoes click on the marble, I was reminded that guests could see me and I was tasked with smiling and serving their needs for the next eight hours. I needed to find my way to the concierge desk and try to fit in. Even more than wanting the guests to like me, I wanted the team to like me. I was the only woman at the concierge desk and the youngest by a decade. As I walked past the same huge floral arrangement from the interview, I felt completely different from the week prior. Cousin Jeffrey, now my colleague, proudly looked on. This was *my* lobby now, and although I was incredibly nervous, it was my opening night, and it was a full house.

During my first week, I noticed that who I was upon arrival and who I became in uniform were two entirely different people. I needed my uniform, or "costume," to give me confidence and credibility behind the concierge desk. It disguised my youthfulness and innocence. It also gave me a voice and the ability to dictate the guests' experience when I would have otherwise had zero authority or insight.

I still needed to get fitted for my real uniform, and Boyds, an upscale department store with an iconic marble staircase located just down the street, knew to expect me. I asked for the store owner upon my arrival. In my faded jean shorts and hooded sweatshirt, I was obviously not their usual customer. As I waited, I glanced at the price tags on the shoes surrounding me. They cost more than my week's pay.

I never expected to be led to the men's department, given a bottle of water, and paired with a tailor who wrapped a tape measure around my waist. I was fitted for two black pantsuits and five white crew neck blouses. Garment bags with my name on them would be hand delivered to the hotel by courier in two weeks. I chuckled, thinking they were stuck with me now.

Back in the Rittenhouse lobby, I got tips from new female coworkers about wearing lipstick and getting a manicure, as my hands would be on constant display when showcasing menus and maps. Black socks and black shoes would complete my look, but I was quickly realizing I didn't have anything suitable to allow me to stand on marble for eight hours. My mom, who was thrilled I would have to wear my hair in some style other than a floppy bun, took me to Aerosoles, the women's comfort-shoe store, but not even their shoes were supportive enough for marble. Two hundred and eighty-five dollars later, a pair of Mephisto Mary Janes were mine. They were the most expensive personal item I'd ever owned. I loved them and the smell of real leather. The break-in period took exactly one shift, and they melded perfectly to my high arches.

"It will be a tax write-off," my mom said.

Business cards were the final accessory. I was shown a proof to sign off on and then forgot about it until a week later when a small cardboard box was dropped on my desk from Estelle in purchasing. It was my first official business card, and holding it in my hands for the first time, seeing my name and title, validated the career trajectory I was now on. Each concierge had their own card holder on the desk we all shared. We also shared one concierge email address. None of this mattered. Nor did my age or inexperience. I was a concierge at the Rittenhouse.

I worked in tandem with Frank Marandino, a man in his mid-forties, who would soon become the chef concierge (the French term for concierge manager). He wore shiny cuff links, had perfectly manicured nails, and showered female guests and residents with double cheek kisses. Next to Frank I felt safe.

But eventually he took a lunch break and I found myself alone at the desk, praying no one would approach. I knew that receiving recommendations from a timid and ambivalent concierge wasn't desirable and heard my dad's classic line "Fake it until you make it" reverberating in my head.

The truth was, in the early weeks, if someone did approach, they most certainly weren't looking for me.

"Is Frank in today?" guests would commonly ask.

"He's on break," I'd say, "but I'd be happy to assist you."

"No, thank you. I'll come back."

I quickly realized that Frank's pedestal status was achievable with hard work and some fabulous acting. He wasn't Mr. Five Diamond outside of work. He grew up in Vineland, New Jersey, and currently lived in a three-bedroom house in the modest suburb of Cherry Hill with his partner and dog. In guest's eyes he was an equal. It was his uniform and life experiences, not his schooling, that gave him confidence and empowered him to serve the guest in the most memorable way he could.

The other concierge, bellmen, and doormen on our team grew up in blue-collar towns themselves. And although being on the receiving end of luxury service was not part of their upbringing, they, too, had learned to turn on the "right this way" human-arrow gesture, along with charm and polish, for paying guests.

Frank effortlessly dished out restaurant recommendations and coordinated guest itineraries, but what he really taught me was the art of the schmooze. Some other hotels might require a concierge to complete as many guest transactions as they can in a shift. Most concierge desks are purposely podiums, not desks, as they don't want to encourage guests' hanging around for too long. But at the Rittenhouse, it was our duty to get to know guests, treat them like they were the only one.

Frank taught me the importance of making genuine

guest connections and getting to know their likes, wants, and needs through friendly dialogue. Where I might have initially said, "Good morning, Mr. and Mrs. Smith. How may I assist you today?" Frank taught me to say, "Good morning, Mr. and Mrs. Smith. How was dinner last evening at Barclay Prime, and which steak knife did you select?"

This type of dialogue also allows you to better personalize future recommendations, which in turn makes guests feel as if they are the only one you are serving. In general, the greater rapport, the greater reward in the form of a sizable gratuity. It also meant the guest would ask for you the next time they returned to Philadelphia. Having someone remember your name and how you made them feel was so rewarding. Or better yet, approaching them first and welcoming them back as they crossed through the lobby on their way to the reception area.

What could be better than creating a memorable experience for a guest and be handsomely rewarded for it? I was hooked.

BE OUR GUEST

Shamus, my favorite doorman, who still looked sun kissed in December, approached our Chrysler Sebring convertible wearing his long black overcoat and uniform hat, and I beamed from the passenger window when he called me "Miss Cooperstein." I was checking in to the Rittenhouse for the night with my longtime boyfriend, Derrick. I hoped it would be romantic, and I was also eager for Derrick to acknowledge just how great the property was that I had been boasting about for the past few months. I wanted him to say that he was proud of me.

As I approached my six-month mark of being a concierge, I made a reservation for my complimentary stay, along with dinner at Lacroix, which had been named "Best New Restaurant" in the United States the year prior. Both the Rittenhouse, which had only ninety-eight guest rooms, and the restaurant, led by Jean-Marie Lacroix, were coveted reservations and cost upward of $1,000 a night combined, a price point that most of the staff, and the rest of the world, would never have been able to afford. Management fortunately saw the value in offering us our own firsthand guest experience.

I wondered as I entered the lobby, *Will I ever be able to afford a night like this ever again?*

Shamus carried our bags to the front desk and gestured for us to follow him to where Rosella, my front desk coworker, was eagerly waiting to walk us through the check-in process. Facing Rosella and having my back to the traffic flow of the lobby, which was usually as entertaining as the boardwalk on a Saturday night in July, was so odd.

Frank looked on and smiled from the concierge desk, two feet to my left. "Welcome, Miss Cooperstein and Mr. Smith," he said. "We have taken the liberty of upgrading you to a park view suite, with an unobstructed view of Rittenhouse Square. Justin will be happy to assist you with your luggage. Have a wonderful stay."

I had heard Rosella recite this script to hundreds of guests before. But being addressed with a title and last name rather than as Jamie, while bellman Justin stood nearby ready to transport our luggage, I felt like I was hearing these words for the first time. I felt special. Before I had even left the lobby, I felt like a true guest and the recipient of genuine hospitality.

We turned around, and Justin gestured toward the elevator bay as if he were meeting us for the first time, even though I knew he was a drummer for a KISS tribute band and we had just the day before gone out for beers and played darts with other fellow employees after work.

"Please, right this way," he said.

In the elevator he referenced the location of Lacroix, the restaurant; Boathouse Row, the bar; Adolf Biecker, the spa; and the fitness center, the pool, and other services. I tried to pretend I wasn't already familiar with the layout or the amenities. I was filled with immense pride as I floated down the hallway and watched Justin insert his key card into our guest room door, ours for the next twenty-four hours.

One significant advantage of working in the front-office department was that my closest colleagues had hand selected our room. Frank also arranged for an in-room amenity of chocolate-covered strawberries. The Rittenhouse guest rooms are grand and full of character and rich fabrics, including white duvets, bold geometric carpeting, and antique furnishings and are far removed from the generic rectangular rooms most people come to expect. The smallest room on the lowest floor would have still been a showstopper, but I wasn't complaining about our direct view of Rittenhouse Square, one city block's worth of green space, walkways, and benches with a fountain in the middle.

Justin continued his tutorial inside the room after he placed our bags on wooden luggage racks. He turned on all the lights for us and showed us how to use the thermostat, which wasn't exactly intuitive. The next time a guest called down to the concierge desk frustrated over the room being too cold, I now knew what to do. I was also able to test out the bath amenities guests would consistently rave about. While in the shower, I found our famous yellow rectangular bar soap, wrapped in cellophane and sealed with a circular gold foil sticker. It was so popular, both due to its clean scent and creamy texture, that guests would stop at the desk to inquire if it was for sale. Derrick, however, while quickly looking up from scrolling on his Blackberry, said he preferred the soap in the men's locker room at Aronimink.

After an afternoon nap—on the 100 percent cotton Italian linens perfectly tucked on the king-size bed—we needed to get dressed for our five-course tasting menu at Lacroix. Derrick wore a suit every day as an attorney, but I rarely had an opportunity to get dressed up, and I took my time using the hair dryer to style my hair in the oversize bathroom.

As we stepped across the threshold of the restaurant, the view of Rittenhouse Square—a panorama of glistening holiday lights—was breathtaking. We were given a table adjacent to the floor-to-ceiling glass windows, which over-hung the driveway below and made us feel as if we were dining in the treetops. I felt like I was inside a snow globe, looking out on a beautiful winter scene.

A server wearing a light-green collared shirt and tie pulled my chair away from the table for me, and I was handed my menu first. This was one of my first fine-dining experiences ever, and certainly the first without my parents, and it was remarkable how many different staff members played a role. They each had a specific job: fill water glasses, take orders, remove plates, change out silverware, educate us on wine, scrape crumbs, and so on. Before this meal, I thought one employee per table was standard.

My favorite part was the synchronized plating of each course and how both Derrick and I would look at each other with excitement when the next course was revealed. The plates filled with a mix of greens and proteins were an artform of contrasting colors and shapes and textures. Sometimes the elements in the dish were so small and manicured in relationship to the size of the plate. Even Derrick, whom I'd never characterize as easily impressed, said, "Wow." The meal lasted for hours, and mid-meal, after I excused myself to go to the restroom, I returned to find my napkin folded beautifully. A Five Diamond moment, executed to look effortless.

The next morning I wanted to call down to the desk for a late checkout to explore the city, but Derrick said he needed to get back to Paoli, a suburb of Philadelphia, to tackle some home repairs. He said goodbye and drove away, and I walked a block home to my new studio apartment while I had the realization that as I was falling in love with the city (and luxury and service), I was falling out of love with him.

The city, full of stores, restaurants, and live theater productions, was ever changing, and I was now its ambassador.

On Monday, back at my desk, I had the confidence of a seasoned veteran. I could speak firsthand about caviar and foie gras when a couple in their sixties inquired at check-in about going to the orchestra and having dinner at Lacroix beforehand.

"I see you are staying with us for two nights," I said, "and I would love to help you make both memorable. Dinner at Lacroix is five courses, and two and a half hours is suggested for the full experience, especially if you enjoy wine pairings. You wouldn't have time to dine beforehand, and dining postshow wouldn't be ideal either. Would you be open to dining at Lacroix tonight instead? If so, I can recommend another phenomenal restaurant with a pretheater menu for tomorrow."

"Oh, wow! That's very helpful." Their eyes lit up, surprised, and appreciative of my plan B.

The old me would have acquiesced and proceeded with jamming too much into one night. I no longer needed to rely on reviews or input from Frank. My overnight stay gave me the firsthand experience of seeing a crumb scraper in action and an understanding of why the check was so high (e.g., food cost plus labor cost). I now knew what it was like to experience turndown service upon a return from dinner, with the curtains drawn, the lighting dim, the clock radio playing soft jazz, slippers placed beside the bed, and a chocolate on the nightstand.

I was inspired to want more luxury experiences. I was also thankful that the Rittenhouse leadership team realized that an immersive overnight stay would encourage team members to remain excited about delivering personalized and proactive service.

For the next week or two, I was on cloud nine: The marble on the floor felt like plush carpet, and I could remain standing forever, poised to say, "My pleasure."

A CULTURAL
AWAKENING

It was becoming increasingly clear that I was the suburban Caucasian kid while our three-hundred-person team was a melting pot of different nationalities, ethnicities, sexual orientations, and socioeconomic backgrounds. Employees spoke twenty-plus different languages, and daily I felt like the odd one out among my coworkers.

I learned by socializing and watching.

Miguel, our steadfast lobby attendant who chatted while he cleaned, was from Argentina.

Rose, our outspoken hotel operator, who boasted that her latest Coach bag was "bought by her sugar daddy," was from Liberia.

David Benton, our proud general manager who made us all stand a little taller, was British.

Olga, a favorite front desk agent, and Marie, our tea-room manager, were both from France, and it was fun to hear Olga request a tea reservation for a guest in French.

Carol, an introverted front desk agent with a high

school diploma, worked side by side with Alicia, who soon entered a PhD program, to teach her how to use the computer system.

Yan, a back-of-house Mandarin-speaking dishwasher, was requested by Lucia, a front-of-house manager, to help assist and translate, while still wearing his apron, for a VIP guest arriving from China.

And I had a surprising rapport with each and every one of the bellmen and doormen who took direction from me—a woman. Justin, my darts partner, caught the bus to work from his childhood home in Roxborough, near the famous Dalessandro's Steaks (cheesesteaks, that is). Timiko, a big teddy bear, lived with his three kids and baby momma in West Philly, adjacent to the zoo, where urban murals replaced graffitied walls. Erik, who commuted from South Jersey, had a degree in international business and a slight Southern twang from going to school in Charleston. Mike S., who was proud to be from a "youse guys" neighborhood in the northeast, had just knocked up his girlfriend. Jono lived with his boyfriend, a frequent visitor, just a few blocks away on a quaint tree-lined street. Mike B., originally from an affluent suburb, obsessed over skateboards and his nose ring, which he tucked up under his nostril while at work. We bonded over sports mostly. And my part-time gig as a left-field ball girl for the Philadelphia Phillies, a job I held for the 2004 and 2005 seasons, was a source of immense bragging rights. I was comfortable being one of the guys again, just like in my days in sports journalism.

I loved them all, the whole team. Everyone mattered. Our team mattered. As different as we were, our backstories didn't divide us—they united us.

My hometown, Broomall, and high school class of 330

were predominantly Caucasian. Most of my friends looked and sounded like me, and they all lived in three- and four-bedroom homes, just like me. College was more of the same. When I would pop into the back office of the hotel to print a boarding pass or get a sleeve of new luggage tags, Rose, although a fan of mine, would remind me frequently, "Your daddy was a dentist and what do you know?"

She was right—I didn't know a lot about a lot. My cultural awareness was just beginning.

I came to appreciate and understand, too, that not everyone found their way to the hotel with a bachelor's degree and no debt. Everyone's story intrigued and inspired me, and I began to notice three distinct types of hotel employees: the Hotel Lifer, Hotel Climber, and Résumé Filler.

Some of my colleagues—like Miguel—were Hotel Lifers and would mop the lobby floors and empty ashtrays for decades to come. The Hotel Lifers excelled in their role and had no desire to "climb the ladder." Plus, if they left to take another job, they'd lose their seniority, preferred schedule, and accrued vacation days. I assumed the small annual pay increases kept them loyal.

Next were the Hotel Climbers, like Lanay, our young and dynamic in-house reservationist. She hadn't finished college and needed a job quickly. She was authentically salesy and made booking reservations at the highest possible rate look easy. Eleven years later she became the director of catering at the Rittenhouse, a coveted position in the industry, curating wedding packages (selling the ballroom, food packages, liquor packages, upgraded linens, etc.) for luxury brides and their demanding moms.

Lastly, we had the Résumé Fillers, like my front desk colleagues Alicia and Ted. They both grew up in privileged households, graduated from private colleges with honors, and were looking to schmooze and build their network. They wanted to surround themselves with highfalutin individuals like rock stars, CEOs, and politicians. Their hourly position was merely a brag-worthy stepping stone before they started a graduate degree. For Ted, it was international marketing. For Alicia, it was psychotherapy. Given their parental support, they didn't really need to work, but they did so because it was socially acceptable.

But which category did I fit in? Would I remain a concierge for decades? I did love it. Would I want to be a hotel general manager some day? Possibly. Or would I pursue a higher degree and segue to a different field? The verdict was still out.

COMFORT ZONE

The Rittenhouse's guests were equally diverse, except for their income bracket, and frequently traveled across multiple time zones before passing through our front doors. We strived to uphold the guiding principles of the United Nations—peace and security—and our team did a phenomenal job making guests feel right at home when they were actually very far from home.

Three things we did routinely as a hotel (and department) made me feel like a proud Philadelphia ambassador:

1. We kept an updated list of current employees and the languages they spoke, like dishwasher Yan and his Mandarin, in the event they might be needed to assist with a warm welcome or step in for necessary translation.
2. We proactively fetched international newspapers for our VIP guests from a local independent bookshop on the University of Pennsylvania campus.

3. We switched out the name plates on our five
    round analog clocks, displayed above the
    reception area, to reflect the cities of select
    in-house guests from other time zones.

Why guests chose the Rittenhouse for their lodging was obvious, but I also became fascinated with why
they chose Philadelphia as a destination at all: Were they
coming for a work meeting? To see historical sights? For a
medical procedure? To visit local colleges? The list goes on.

My curiosity got me considering a career in destination marketing—or marketing Philadelphia as an attractive destination for the leisure traveler—and in September
2005, I began pursuing my master's in hospitality and
tourism at Temple University, chipping away at courses
one at a time. When I had some downtime at the end of
a quiet 3:00–11:00 p.m. shift at the Rittenhouse, I would
pull out a textbook and turn my attention to the required
reading, knowing the hospitality education I was receiving
at the hotel was far more valuable. Temple no doubt had a
fantastic program—it was the only hospitality program I
applied for, in fact—but more than the academic lessons
learned, what was great about Temple was that it pushed
me out of my comfort zone.

That is, though the university was less than an hour
away from the little Philly suburb I grew up in, it felt like a
world apart to me. I had first caught a glimpse of that world
during my Fox 29 internship, when I recorded game footage from a Temple men's basketball game at the Liacouras
Center, the sports arena in the heart of campus. My jaw
flew open, and I clutched the side of the news van as we approached Broad Street and Cecil B. Moore Avenue, a part

of Philadelphia I had never seen outside a newscast, where it was usually highlighted as a crime-ridden zip code. Other than the cherry red *T* flags (that's *T* for *Temple*) waving along North Broad Street, I was surrounded by blighted buildings and the weathered faces of those who had experienced great hardship. A subway station was located directly outside the arena, and I had never experienced SEPTA in any facet before, let alone below ground in a rough-and-tumble neighborhood.

Though I didn't know it at the time, both the Rittenhouse and Temple were the perfect places for a kid like me—a kid with a growing urgency to meet people different from me, to explore, to see what else was out there.

And some of what I saw shocked me.

ADDICTION, PORN, AND PROSTITUTES

Stepping foot into the hotel industry was a wake-up call to the not-always-sunny real world and the choices some people make. It was a jarring experience for this self-proclaimed good girl who'd lived in a padded bubble mailer her whole life.

I had never tried drugs of any kind, for instance. My one and only cigarette was smoked in a parking lot while pregaming before a Jimmy Buffet concert one summer home from college. And I had had sex with only one partner by the time I became a concierge. To me, rebelling had meant throwing back one too many red solo cups of keg beer at a frat party with my college besties.

The Rittenhouse, however, exposed me to subjects mostly foreign to me—addiction, porn, and prostitutes among them. That paddled-bubble-mailer version of me? It didn't last for long.

THE ADDICT

My concierge colleague Simon's hands were shaking. Wildly. It seemed like he had no control over them either. We were standing shoulder to shoulder behind the concierge desk, and it was hard to not stare. I also smelled an Altoids mint, the strong kind, and heard him crunch it, which was odd because in the service industry, we were not supposed to have anything in our mouths. His large calloused hands kept opening the tin for another little mint, again and again.

At first I thought Simon—who, while only in his early thirties, had a weathered and sun-kissed complexion, as if he worked in construction—had a fresh-breath fetish or an oral fixation. But his hands began to shake more routinely. Some days they tremored so much he would become self-conscious and feel the need to apologize. His face would bead with perspiration, and early on I just thought he found the lobby too warm.

He also smelled of stale booze.

One day Simon didn't show up for work, and when Frank finally got a hold of him twenty-four hours later, the staff let out a sigh of relief. With Frank's encouragement, human resources placed Simon on disability so he could seek out treatment, effective immediately. He never returned, and I never got to say goodbye after working closely with him for the better part of a year. And to this day, I still think of him when I see or smell a tin of Altoids.

THE HYPED-UP BELLMAN

Drug tests were not a condition of employment at the Rittenhouse. This had ramifications, both good and bad. Good because our talented front-of-house and back-of-house teams could enjoy some recreational weed. Bad because we inadvertently hired a junkie bellman.

Our bell staff was seasoned, and we rarely had turnover. But every once in a while, we needed to add someone to the team. Evan, with purposefully messy spikes atop his head, looked like he could front the band Blink-182. At his interview he was charming and personable, and I was excited for him to join our department. That is until I saw, on his very first shift, his bloodshot eyes and the pattern of his jumpy, pacing, always-moving, always-interrupting behavior. Evan was so overly energetic that he was unable to remain posted in the lobby, where bellmen are required to stand. I'd never seen someone this hyped up outside of a rock concert. The other bellmen began to complain during his training shift, and luckily for us, he hadn't been paired one on one with any guests yet.

"He's high on cocaine," some suggested.

Frank took Evan into the back office and laid into him. "You are an embarrassment!" he screamed. "Are you for real? It's a good thing that David Benton, our general manager, is off today!"

By week's end Evan had become a distant memory.

THE ADULT-MOVIE LOVER

During the week, the Rittenhouse relied on business travelers to fill its rooms, and the hotel benefited from pre-negotiated corporate room rates with a variety of large companies in the region. The room charge and tax were almost always covered by the corporation on behalf of the guest, but rarely were incidental charges included.

Rosella, the assistant front-office manager, shared with me one day in the back office that in-room porn was the top incidental charge. She pulled a report of in-house guests and their movie selections and snickered.

"Look at how many . . ." she said.

I couldn't believe it. If I were a business traveler, I would be ordering room service or raiding the minibar.

Before smart TVs and streaming services—and well before iPhones and iPads—hotels subscribed to an in-room movie-subscription service that provided guests with a menu of viewing choices, charged à la carte. Porn had a higher price tag, about ten dollars more than a classic like *Forrest Gump*. When Rosella reviewed the incidental charges with each guest at checkout and mentioned the $18.99 charge was for an in-room movie, we all knew the guest had taken matters into their own hands the night before. It was hard not to smirk when standing only two feet to the right of the front desk.

"Oh, that's strange, I didn't order a movie," a businessman, almost always in his forties or fifties, would claim. Or they'd claim that they didn't realize there was an additional charge. They were flat-out lying, but frequent travelers know that if they politely question a charge, it will get removed from their bill, no questions asked.

Of course, during this dispute, they didn't know we knew their choice of movie. I will never know how the front desk agents kept a straight face after witnessing so many men deny that they ordered porn. I swore I would make sure my future husband didn't have to travel for work.

THE HIRED PROSTITUTE

Weekends brought a whole new type of clientele—leisure guests—and sometimes they invited a scantily clad lady friend. I'm sure the overnight staff, specifically night manager Anthony and night butlers Charles and Preston, had more exposure to the comings and goings of this specific guest population. But for me this was something I had been exposed to only on television when Julia Roberts named her hourly price while she and Richard Gere sped off in a Lotus. It sometimes felt like I, too, had been cast in a movie.

Fortunately, prostitutes had no interest in engaging with the front desk or concierge staff. It was actually the last place you'd find them. Their goal was to keep a low profile and find their desired room destination as swiftly as they could. Ironically, while enrolled in my hospitality-law class, I learned that a hotel had the legal right to turn away certain types of guests—those with a communicable disease, someone unwilling to pay, someone who is an unreasonable danger to others, or someone attempting to use the room for an unlawful purpose. Although prostitution was illegal in Pennsylvania, it was just business as usual at the Rittenhouse because (a) we couldn't really prove unlawful activity without bearing witness to the exchange of payment for it, and (b) no one wanted to accuse a guest of such a thing.

Even without an accusation, it could still be incredibly awkward. Our elevators weren't on a fob system, and any "guest" that arrived could earnestly walk through the lobby and quietly escape upstairs undetected.

Except when Rosella was on duty.

Once, we were nearing the end of the 3:00–11:00 p.m. shift, and from my usual spot behind the desk, I watched her approach two out-of-place women in heeled boots, who appeared to be lost. Their long coats were left open ever so slightly in the front, leaving little to the imagination.

"Good evening, ladies," Rosella said. "Can I help you with anything?"

"We are trying to locate room 614. Mr. Smith is expecting us."

"I will let him know you've arrived. Who may I tell him is here?"

They gave Rosella their names, and with a devilish gleam in her eye, she announced them over the phone to Mr. Smith.

She winked at me, and my jaw dropped.

Mr. Smith clearly had no idea of his guests' names, only that he had requested their arrival. Rosella walked them to the elevator and pushed the button for the sixth floor.

We really do treat every guest like a VIP, I remarked to Rosella afterward. Even when it can be so easy to pass judgment.

"We are here to serve," she said.

I scratched my head in disbelief over this new education I was receiving—it, like so many other lessons, was far more valuable than my Temple coursework.

When my parents would ask how the job was going, I'd tell them, "Never a dull moment."

SPEED DIAL

Never dull indeed. Outlandish guest scenarios and requests happened routinely, in fact, and I never knew whether to laugh or cry. But our job—as Rosella had so wisely said—was to serve, so I put my head down, despite my feet killing me, and got to work.

Two of those laugh-or-cry requests were phone calls.

BOTOX BRIDE

"I'm in a pickle," a young woman told me over the phone. "I need help! I'm headed to Philly tomorrow for my wedding this weekend, and I wasn't able to get a Botox appointment here in Florida. Do you know where to get one?"

I panicked. *What's Botox?*

I took a deep breath, like Frank taught me. "That's a great question. Let me find out the answer for you! May I please put you on hold for a moment?"

I googled: *Botox.* I read: "A series of injections to the face to erase wrinkles." Back then, Botox was not mainstream and had only just received FDA approval for cosmetic use. A cosmetic medical procedure seventy-two hours before her wedding! *Whom do I call and ask?* I was glad I had the luxury of a hold button. *The bell staff? No. Rose or Lanay in the back office?* Both were on the phone.

I came back on the line. "Can I confirm a good contact number for you? I will make some inquiries and will get back to you later today."

I leaned over to Maureen—in her forties, a mom of three, the least vain person in our department and the most gentle and kind—and asked where to get an appointment.

"She's in luck," Maureen said. "There's a plastic surgery office on the third floor."

Jackpot!

I called the bride back. "Good news," I relayed. "Copit & Moore has an office in the Rittenhouse, and they can accommodate you upon your arrival. They prefer for you to call them directly to go through a few necessary pre-screening questions. May I give you their number?"

"Thank you," she said, the relief in her voice crystal clear.

I wondered if her future spouse knew about the up-coming treatment.

Two days later, I met the sun-kissed, thirtysomething bride—a perfectly highlighted blond with a lovely complexion. She thanked me again for securing the appointment.

I smiled. "My pleasure."

But all I could think was *I'm not going. I'm not going*—a phrase we said to ourselves to detach from absurd requests. She was a beautiful young woman. A beautiful young woman with toxins in her face.

BEANIE BABIES OR BUST

"Hi, Jamie," said a middle-aged female guest through the phone. "I'm a collector of Beanie Babies. You know, the colorful, bean-filled animal friends?"

"Yes, I'm familiar," I said. "My sister used to collect them. How can I help you?" I imagined the tub my sister and I had in our room and our trips to Hallmark stores to buy them.

"Well, I'm looking to add to my collection, and I was hoping you could map out a few specialty stores that might sell rare Beanie Babies."

"Rare?"

"Yes. I'm on the hunt for the brown moose, the chicken, and the spotted dog. These are so hard to find—impossible, actually—and I was hoping you might be able to point me in the right direction."

Beanie Babies hadn't been a thing since the late nineties. Also, the height of the craze had brought many counterfeits. This wasn't an easy task.

I made an effort to avoid overpromising. "I'd be happy to generate a list of specialty toy and antique shops in the Philadelphia area," I said. "I would be unable to confirm inventory or authenticity, but I can provide you with the store hours, a telephone number, and a map."

Like with every guest, I genuinely wished her luck but knew, due to shift work, I'd probably never speak with her again.

I wanted to know if she returned to the hotel with a stuffed moose in a plastic case. How many stores had she gone to? How much had she paid?

That's the plight of a concierge: rarely having closure with guests and learning about their experience. Frequently I would provide a guest with a great weekend itinerary, and if I was off on Sunday when they were due to check out, I wouldn't have any way to close the loop. It felt like reading a mystery novel with the last page ripped out. I often yearned for the conclusion, some closure, a note from the guest—even more than a gratuity. True fulfillment came with the validation that someone had had a good time or a successful dinner or outing. How had their story ended?

One of my favorite things was to return to the hotel after a couple of days off to find an envelope with my name on it, filled with a five-, ten-, or twenty-dollar bill. But the best compensation was both the cash and a handwritten note, such as this one:

> *Dear Jamie,*
>> *We loved our dinner at Amada.*
>> *Thank you so much again for securing us a table. You were right, their garlic shrimp was outstanding! Hope to see you upon our return to Philadelphia.*
>> *Fondly,*
>> *The Lee Family*

A pat on the back, an acknowledgment of the expertise I cared so deeply about. Making a reservation felt less like a transaction and more like an opportunity to find small ways to personalize the experience and ask questions about dietary restrictions, table preference, and so on—an intimacy in which I listened and tried to paint an accurate picture. For the Lee family, that intimacy resulted in a memorable meal between them and an Iron Chef.

I lived for moments such as these—moments that, as I moved deeper into my Rittenhouse tenure, were fewer than I'd like.

WEDDED BLISS
AND BURNOUT

Few moments—or series of moments—captured my growing disenchantment better than near-nonstop lavish weddings at the Rittenhouse most Friday and Saturday nights.

I began to feel as if I were starring in *Groundhog Day*, every weekend on repeat—especially during peak wedding season. A different bride and groom, different family, different religion, but the same ballroom setup, same wedding cake designers, same maître d'. And the same boisterous wedding party reunion: parents, siblings, bridesmaids, groomsmen, matriarchs, patriarchs, uncles, aunts, cousins, and friends, all taking over the entire hotel for the duration of the weekend.

Every Jewish wedding happened on Saturdays after sundown. Every cocktail hour displayed a sushi bar and ice sculpture. Every reception featured a nine-piece band and female lead singer belting "At Last" by Etta James. Every ceremony had a rotation of top-of-the-line florists, photographers, and videographers. And if Jewish, a grand chuppah laced with hydrangeas. And everybody checked out on Sunday, glowing and tired.

Though exhausting and repetitive, it was a joy to be a small part of someone's big day, which almost always began the same way. Early in the sales cycle, the director of catering, Rema—a big, curvy, and often intimidating Italian from South Philly—shared with potential clients the Rittenhouse's minimum fee for a Saturday-night affair: $75K. Few blinked at the price tag, and no one questioned Rema. Ever.

Afterward she toured the impeccably dressed bride and her mother, and sometimes her father (but rarely the groom), throughout the ballroom, guest room suites, salon, and concierge desk, where it was our job to dote and say all the right things. Then, in an effort to close the deal with a mother of the bride, Rema would offer up our desk as a one-stop shop. Since a sense of entitlement often accompanied a sizable bill, this cherry-on-top perk would lead to many wedding-related requests passing through our desk. We happily obliged with Five Diamond services:

- tuxedo rental
- last-minute shopping trips for misplaced cuff links
- gift bags with Goldenberg's peanut chews and soft pretzels for the out-of-town guests
- a list of what to do in Philly that weekend
- private trolley transportation
- rehearsal dinner recommendations and reservations
- spa, nails, blowouts
- childcare

The buildup to the day was systematic and practical. But I learned, come the big day, most weddings come with big feelings. Since I had no chair, I stood at my desk fielding frantic calls from members of the wedding party.

"Help! I lost my cuff links!"

"Help! I stepped on my gown, and it ripped!"

Help. Help. Help.

I called it *triage*, putting out fires and fixing things at the last minute. The most peaceful thirty minutes of the day was during the second-floor ceremony.

Then, 250 people would descend into the Mary Cassatt Tea Room for the cocktail hour, twenty feet from the concierge desk. On a Saturday night, I became a voyeur into a raucous sixty minutes of butlered hors d'oeuvres consumption. The sea of people was packed so tightly I often wondered how the waitstaff navigated. Sometimes women, drink in hand, would wander over.

"Can you hold my purse or pashmina?" they'd ask.

"Yes," I would say over the roar of the crowd as I accommodated their requests.

Meanwhile, upstairs, the housemen, banquet servers, and preferred vendors had sixty minutes to frantically set up the reception, relocating chairs from the ceremony space to the ballroom. The maître d' rang a triangle to encourage the crowd to make their way back upstairs. Once the parade left the lobby, it was peaceful again.

I'd never have expected it would be the tuxedos that would make me raise my nose. Since the hotel encouraged it, on the day of checkout the groomsmen dropped off their dirty tuxedos at the desk, and we stored them in the bell closet until Monday morning, when the rental company picked them up. With a smile, I carried smelly garment bags full of smoke residue, sweat, and stains back and forth to the bell closet.

On Saturdays, Sundays, and Mondays, I waved good-bye to the happy bride and groom with appropriate fanfare after their requested late checkout, and the staff was left to tend to the soiled linens, vacuum, scrub, break down tables, and stack chairs, only to do it all again the following weekend.

When I'd first read my job description, I'd mistak-enly focused on the glam: booking hard-to-come-by din-ner reservations, theater tickets, massages, and limos for the appreciative recipient. But a year into my Rittenhouse tenure, I found myself consumed by dry cleaning and shined-shoe collection, booking afternoon tea reserva-tions, assisting with safe deposit box storage, selling hotel gift certificates, faxing documents, storing and procuring luggage from the bell closet (in the absence of a bellman), and hauling stinky wedding tuxedos.

As a college graduate who'd once dreamed of a splashy broadcasting career, I was humbled by the work. No mat-ter how big or small, glamorous or mundane, we still had to find a way to make the guest (and their request) feel like our top priority. Not only was the sexiness I'd imagined absent, but I often rolled my eyes over the simplicity of the tasks.

In the mid-2000s, for instance, every passenger had to print their boarding pass at home before leaving for the airport. On a busy shift, I got requests to print up to twenty of them. I memorized the home pages and neces-sary data fields for each requested airline and learned to complete the task in seconds. When a guest called with their request, I folded their boarding pass, placed it in an envelope, and wrote their name and room number on it for collection at the front desk.

Southwest Airlines' entry into the Philadelphia market presented an added challenge at the concierge desk. Their attractive fares and playful customer service had created an instant loyal following, but the unique seating situation with Southwest meant we had to print boarding passes exactly twenty-four hours from the flight departure time to ensure our guests made it into the first boarding group. With other airlines, I would try to print the pass whenever the request came in. I could no longer do that. The time sensitivity of Southwest's check-in meant I had to set a timer, drop whatever I was doing for another guest, and print the pass. My competitive spirit made me strive to get within the first five people (A 1–5) to board the plane. I began to find ways to make even printing a boarding pass seem exciting. If I accomplished the task to the best of my ability and with a genuine smile, I had succeeded.

But the more boarding passes I printed, the more paper cuts I walked home with every night—and the more I began to realize that at some point I'd need more than the Rittenhouse.

A THIRTY-THREE-STORY MYSTERY

The "more" I was thinking about began to take shape when I stood in the Rittenhouse's Carrara-marble lobby thinking about what was above the thirteenth floor. What did it look like?

I knew the twenty floors above the hotel were filled with some of the most expensive real estate in town, but the residents had their own entrance, lobby, elevator bay, and residential staff. They even had their own dedicated condo manager, Scott, who wore a dark suit and always said yes. He had to figure out how to exceed the expectations of an affluent group of retirees, including many widows, who had time to scrutinize every inch. However, when residents came to the hotel side to access the gym, pool, spa, and restaurants, which were shared with guests, they also benefited from our concierge services.

Back then we sold postage stamps at the concierge desk. Mail was collected on-site, so to offer stamps to residents in the dead of winter was a big convenience. However, one day, Mrs. Fisher, eightysomething, in a London Fog coat asked for "three postcard stamps."

"I'm so sorry, Mrs. Fisher," I said. "Unfortunately, it looks like we have only first-class stamps left. Will those do?"

"No, I'll take a walk to the post office instead."

She pivoted and walked out.

A half hour later, she walked back in and waved while holding the waxed envelope from the post office.

I waved back, smiling, calculating her savings of forty-two cents.

"I guess this is how she saved up enough to live here," Frank said with a grin when I shared the story with him.

I was torn between thinking Mrs. Fisher's choice didn't make sense and respecting her frugality. Either way, it was a reminder that having wealth doesn't mean you need to flaunt it and that maybe I, too, could live at the Rittenhouse if I saved up enough pennies.

Another resident, Mrs. Anderson, an unassuming baby boomer who had her dark-gray hair pulled off her face, would pop down to the lobby at the very end of a shift, always after 9:00 p.m., and ask for photocopy assistance. I guessed she came at night because she knew the administrative staff would be using the copier during the day. She knew the lobby would be quiet and we'd have the time to step away and help her. This routine of copying recipes, records, newspaper clippings, and the like went on most nights I was on the evening shift. I started to wonder if Mrs. Anderson, who was a widow, was equally in need of evening companionship as she was photocopying services. She never tipped.

Residents also liked to use the hotel's house car, a shiny

S-Class Mercedes sedan, even though they had their own dedicated house car, one driven by their own residential staff. Ours was supposed to be off limits for residents. But inevitably there would be times when the residence-condo car was being serviced or in high demand and a hopeful resident like Mrs. Gardner would don an impish smile and stand in front of me.

"Jamie, I see the hotel car is out front," she said. "Ours isn't available. Can Bernard give me a lift?"

In hospitality an alternative to a no is necessary. I wanted to say, "No, no, no," and recite policy. But instead I said, "Yes, Mrs. Gardner. Head to Bernard at the front door, and he can hail a taxi for you."

"A taxi!" she said, flailing her arms, in a fur coat. "Is Frank here? He always says yes."

Control over the car was a constant source of anxiety, and it required a split-second decision each time a resident made an inquiry. The bellman doubled as our hotel driver, and if a resident was being transported in our car when the Johnson, Rodriguez, and Cohen families all arrived within minutes of each other, that meant three full carts of luggage and possibly only one bellman left to assist. We couldn't let people wait for their bags.

When inquiries were made, I prayed our car would be in use and it would be an easy "I'm sorry." The hardest decision was when the car was visibly parked out front. I would get eye rolls from the bell staff, too, who considered me saying no as akin to being robbed of making twenty dollars. They took it personally, and that made me feel so shitty, even if I was making the right decision from the perspective of the guests, who were my primary responsibility.

The more often residents were told yes by Frank, the lead concierge, the more they kept asking. He saw it as a win-win and said yes nine times out of ten. If he accommodated Mrs. Gardner, one of the bellmen would receive a fat gratuity, and Frank's holiday bonus, compiled by the residents, would exponentially increase. All he had to do was make sure David Benton didn't find out.

Mr. Benton, the Rittenhouse's general manager, frequently asked after the whereabouts of the car when doing a daily exterior hotel inspection. If I said, "We took a guest to the Liberty Bell," he nodded in agreement. If I said, cringing, "We took Mrs. Johnson from unit 2702 to get a pedicure," he slapped the desk and marched into the back to find Lucia, the front-office manager. Trying to please the resident, the bellman, the guest, and hotel management all at once was truly impossible. Please the resident, piss off management—and possibly inconvenience the guest. Please management, piss off both the resident and the bellman.

I was a rule follower, and I was okay saying no to a gratuity because I wanted to do the right thing. I liked matters that were stress-free, black and white. But one of the many lessons I learned behind the desk was that when I was on duty and in control, I had to own the decision I was making in the moment. I stood my ground, like with Mrs. Gardner. No amount of pleading, exasperated groans, or foot stomping would alter the outcome.

Until the day I found myself in the elevator going up to the twenty-third floor to help Eleanor, a widow in her mid-seventies, with her computer. I had never engaged with a resident beyond the confines of the concierge desk—my turf.

When I exited the elevator onto residential turf, I immediately noticed the absence of the hotel fixtures. The hallway had a completely different look and feel—mezuzahs at the doors, welcome mats, umbrella stands, door hardware, light fixtures, and carpeting—all different from the guest hallways.

I was nervous, and I couldn't picture what Eleanor looked like as I knocked on her door.

"Welcome. Come on in," she said. "My computer is in the bedroom."

What surprised me on the short walk to the bedroom was that her condo was rather plain, filled with family pictures and tchotchkes. The unobstructed view of flowers blooming in Rittenhouse Square almost stopped me in my tracks. The famous angled windows, found in all the hotel rooms, were still there, but the familiar hotel furnishings and the Rittenhouse logo were not.

In her bedroom, Eleanor's computer was on a desk across from the foot of the bed. Her queen bed, with just a white coverlet, looked plain in comparison to the luxurious satin shams found on the hotel side. Eleanor needed help making sure her computer had virus protection. She also hoped to feel more comfortable using Microsoft Word to compose letters to mail to her granddaughter at overnight camp or to upload and organize photos from her many trips with Stu, her white-haired "friend" and second-act life partner.

Eleanor and Stu traveled the globe together after a chance meeting in a hot-air balloon over Kenya in 1996. I helped them upload photos from trips to Moscow, Beijing, the Amazon, Papua New Guinea, Patagonia, and the North Pole. I loved how progressive they were—not just with their adventurous travels but also by living together unwed in their late seventies and practicing different religions from one another. She was Jewish. He was not. It didn't matter. His sense of humor and positive outlook on life were infectious, and I almost forgot I was being paid to spend time with them.

I envied the pair and their travels, a stark contrast to my grandparents and me, who had never left North America. I didn't even get a passport until later that year. Hearing Eleanor and Stu's stories firsthand as we sifted through photos from their trips was aspirational. Besides yearning to go to Spain, I longed to stay with them for lunch and soak up the wisdom that comes from cultural understanding and visits to so many countries. I began to imagine forging a similar path in my retirement years, with a like-minded future husband.

Although the rapport I developed with Eleanor and Stu while still being "the help" was new, it awakened something inside me, that desire for more. They took the time to get to know me and welcome me into their home as if I were a member of the family, a granddaughter. I strongly preferred this type of in-depth conversation and personalized service to the more surface chitchat I had in the lobby with transient customers.

The inspiration for my next career move was getting stronger.

ROOKIE OF THE YEAR

Repeat guests and residents always asked the same question: "Is Frank here?"

"No, he's off today," I'd say. Or "No, he's at lunch."

Day in and day out—Frank, Frank, Frank.

I wanted guests to light up when they saw me behind the desk, not just ask for Frank. To build my credibility and feed my growing inspiration to up my game and seek more, I would often walk the neighborhood so I could better describe sites, businesses, restaurants, and attractions. If someone asked for the best gelato in town, I said, "Two blocks over," and guided them using landmarks to Capogiro's delicious seasonal flavors. During my time off, I flashed my business card to museums, restaurants, stores, and women's boutiques to build relationships and increase my knowledge. It was a smart move, because the perks poured in:

- Taking a hard-hat tour of the Please Touch Museum in its new location at Memorial Hall, which had originally been built in 1876

to celebrate the hundredth birthday of the
United States.

- Enjoying the sticky, fork-tender pomegran-
ate lamb shoulder at Zahav, in their private
dining room.
- Watching a Cirque du Soliel performance
under the grand tent erected at the corner of
Broad and Washington Streets.
- Walking to and from different Stephen Starr
restaurants each December during the holiday
dine-around, where we'd have an appetizer,
an entrée, and a dessert, each at separate
restaurants.
- Obtaining two tickets to every single musi-
cal or play that came to the Walnut Street
Theatre. My mom loved *Mamma Mia*.
- Sitting in Verizon Hall, home of the
Philadelphia Orchestra, for the very first time
and receiving a behind-the-scenes tour of the
Kimmel Center.
- Enjoying the cheese cart and overall Five
Diamond opulence at Le Bec-Fin, which
was at one time rated America's top French
restaurant.
- Standing after-hours beneath the legendary
Macy's Christmas Light Show, narrated by
Julie Andrews, a Philadelphia holiday tradi-
tion since 1956.
- Walking to and from boutique stores during a
Where Magazine–hosted advertiser showcase.
- Seeing previews of blockbuster exhibits—
Body Worlds at the Franklin Institute and

Salvador Dali at the Philadelphia Museum
of Art.
• Laughing hysterically up front at Helium
Comedy Club.

I thanked each and every business and tried my best to promote them when the right opportunity presented itself.

Not only did I not pay a cent for these perks, but the businesses sometimes compensated me too.

Although it felt unethical to receive a kickback from a preferred vendor, Frank said it was permissible, but only if the payout didn't influence my recommendation. This was a slippery slope, especially since vendors were preestablished before my arrival, such as our preferred limousine company and florist. There might be better options out there, and if there were, would I dare speak up?

Both our limousine company and florist generously rewarded our loyal business. Nick, the proprietor of our limo company, handed me hundreds of dollars in cash every two weeks, usually 20 percent of the booking price and tax exempt. At first taking money from Nick felt awkward, but Frank assured me this was par for the course.

If you book a twenty-passenger party bus for a half-day trip to Atlantic City versus a sedan to PHL, the difference was a commission of over a hundred dollars more for the same amount of work. Cash payouts were also made for coordinating trolley-tour sales, in-room massage bookings, and private tours of the historic district or Brandywine Valley. Restaurants paid in dining dollars or dinners. Making rent wouldn't happen with just my $10.50-per-hour paycheck, and under-the-table exchanges such as these were ethical as long as the cash didn't influence my recommendations.

But how could it not?

"Johnny, it's Frank from the Rittenhouse," I overheard one day. "Favor to ask you. I have a new protégé at the desk, and I need Jamie to experience your sensational menu for herself. May she come in for dinner tomorrow night at 6:00 p.m.?"

I thought, *Wow. Look at the power Frank has! One phone call and voilà! A dinner for two.*

I called my grandmother on the walk home from work. "I'd like to take you to Il Portico," I said, "the most elegant Italian restaurant on Rittenhouse Row."

"Wow. Really?"

Yes, really. Soon we were savoring mushrooms, gnocchi, risotto, and tiramisu, and when calculating the tip, I realized I could now treat family and friends to a $150 meal.

The next day, my grandmother called. "Thank you. Dinner was delicious. I couldn't stop raving to my friends at our mah-jongg game this afternoon."

"I had the best evening too! Let's do it again soon!" I told her, knowing I could.

Twenty-four hours later, when a couple asked for a romantic Italian restaurant within walking distance of the hotel, I said, "Il Portico! The gnocchi and tiramisu are incredible."

Eventually I had tasted most prix fixe menus—three to seven courses, including cheeses, pasta, meats, salad, soup, and the raw bar, plus wine pairings—had seen numerous openings of blockbuster exhibits at the Philadelphia Museum of Art, was attending previews five times a year at the Walnut Street Theatre, and knew every inch of and fact about Citizens Bank Park, the new home of the Philadelphia Phillies.

It took only one good interaction (like educating someone about the obstructing pillars in the parquet section at the Academy of Music) for the residents and repeat guests to ask, "What are your thoughts, Jamie?"

I walked the lobby feeling like I had blossomed into an in-the-know concierge who'd found her calling.

TRAPPED

Smoke, smoke, smoke—smoke everywhere.

Fellow employees smoked outside, and guests smoked in the lobby. It seemed like everyone was a smoker. In the afternoons I stood at the podium and got it from all sides. Suddenly I felt like I worked at a bar. My eyes watered, and I tried not to scrunch up my face and cough when international travelers and wedding guests walked up to me while they exhaled a foot from my face and onto my polyester suit and freshly washed hair.

At first I thought my poor achy feet would be the most difficult element of the job, but breathing secondhand smoke made me feel like I was suffocating. And unfortunately most of my tenure at the hotel overlapped with the last years of the smoking-indoors era.* Ashtrays were discreetly placed near the reception area, the lounge, the Mary Cassatt Tea Room, and the front doors. There had to be twelve ashtrays scattered within a space the size of a

---

* The Philadelphia Clean Indoor Air Worker Protection Law passed in 2006, and by 2008 the entire state of Pennsylvania had banned smoking in most indoor public places.

two-bedroom apartment, and day in and day out, I stood in a solid cloud of smoke.

Smith & Wollensky, a popular chain steakhouse, was connected to the lobby, and they allowed smoking at the bar, which was a mere twenty feet from my desk. During Monday Night Football, like clockwork, a guy in an Eagles jersey sauntered over at halftime, blew smoke into my face, and said, "Where can I grab a nightcap?" I'd smile, lean back, and think, *Is halftime over yet? Get away!*

However, I wanted to be that Five Diamond, go-to, in-the-know concierge I'd been working so hard to become. So as tempting as it was to just point him toward Denim Lounge around the corner and swiftly free myself from further dialogue, I'd ask instead, "Are you looking for bottle service or a dance floor? TVs to watch other games or live music?"

Most evenings hotel guests would wander into the lobby, drink in hand, cigarette lit, tipsy, and ask, "How long has this hotel been here?" or "Who is the artist that painted those paintings?" or "Where can I get a cheesesteak?" or "Is there a strip club you'd recommend?"

I'd answer as best I could, open my desk drawer, and pull out a discount card to Delilah's with complimentary admission, all while thinking, *Put me back on the 7:00 a.m. shift.*

Walking home in the dark at 11:15 p.m., reeking of smoke, I felt my desire for more become increasingly clear. Despite the perks and glamour, I'd think, *I can't breathe, and I can't keep doing this.*

FIVE DIAMOND

David Benton's footsteps echoed loudly on the lobby's marble floor. When he rounded the far pillar coming from the executive office, I would jump to attention as if he were my commander and I was lining up for morning roll call.

Mr. Benton was about five foot nine, and the combination of his British accent, his serious expression, and the way his tailored suits fit against his stocky frame demanded excellence. His eye was on everyone at all times. My shoulders would tighten as he approached, but I knew he brought out the best in me. I always wanted to impress him and be on the receiving end of his praise.

When I rested my foot on the file drawer behind the concierge stand, he pointed at it and said, "Foot down, please. Watch your posture." If my name tag was crooked or, worse, if I'd forgotten to put it on, he'd say, "Name tag." Even Lucia, my boss, who had worked with him since 1989, took his direction very seriously. He corrected us, told us to focus on the guest, and encouraged us to keep busy when too many of us were standing around.

Before Thanksgiving Mr. Benton would hand out

turkeys to every employee. On Christmas he would visit the hotel and thank employees on those shifts for their hard work and dedication. At company holiday parties, bashes thrown in the grand ballroom, he would go table to table putting his arm around the backs of housekeepers and engineers, spending more time with hourly workers than his own executive team. And he consistently freed up his schedule to be present during the biweekly new-employee orientation to welcome the newest members of the team and share his wisdom with a drawing on an easel:

His only instruction was as follows: Without lifting your pen from the page, please connect all the dots using the fewest number of straight lines.

The first time I saw and engaged in the exercise, I drew a line. Wrong.

I drew another one. Wrong again. Eventually he showed us the correct solution.

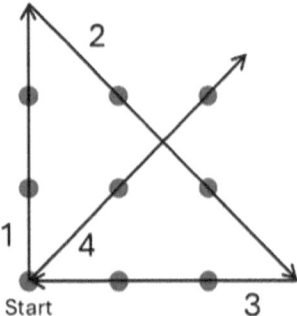

I didn't expect that he would relate this exercise to a guest interaction. He explained that we must do whatever is necessary to please the guest, and sometimes this means thinking outside the box. He encouraged us to think big, to have a voice.

The first time I experienced that exercise was the first time I'd ever been given the power to think big. Afterward, when I walked back to my desk, I knew what was necessary for me to be Five Diamond—take ownership, make decisions—and I decided one of the first things I'd do was to send a complimentary plate of chocolate-covered strawberries to a guest I knew would like them. In truth, despite occasional on-the-job annoyances and my growing eagerness to branch out and seek greener pastures, Mr. Benton and the influential model of excellence he set was a large part of what kept me at the Rittenhouse day after day.

In addition to Mr. Benton's presence, waiting for the arrival of the undercover American Automobile Association (AAA) inspector made me extremely nervous. The inspector's job was to look at both the physical attributes of the hotel, such as furnishings, bedding, technology, and landscaping, and the service being provided by each customer-facing department, including our food-and-beverage outlets and the spa. The inspector's word would single-handedly determine the rating and reputation of the Rittenhouse for the next calendar year.

Fortunately, during my tenure, each spring we were reawarded the coveted Five Diamond status, an accolade given to fewer than 0.05 percent of properties in North America. In Philadelphia only one other hotel—the Four Seasons—reached Five Diamond status. It was as difficult to win as the Heisman Trophy.

Lucia and Rosella, the front-office leadership team, scrutinized any and all reservations made by phone with our in-house reservations team, to see if they met the initial criteria for a possible inspector—solo traveler, not affiliated with a corporate booking or in-house meeting or event, and a one- or two-night reservation. What I loved was the goal: to figure out who the potential inspector was before they stepped foot on-site.

For me, this meant being extra vigilant: wearing a freshly pressed uniform consisting of a black suit and white crew neck blouse with a name tag and keeping a genuine smile on my face. I also made sure to use the guest's name, insert the time of day in my greetings, escort guests when directions were requested, and ask, "Is there anything else I can assist with?" at the end of each guest conversation. I made a conscious effort to be extra polished with my communication, removing my local slang (e.g., "No problem. Have a good one!" and instead using "My pleasure. Have a wonderful day!"). I anticipated guests' needs and offered them personalized service knowing I would be under review as well.

I couldn't let myself be caught off guard for a single moment. Being on display for eight hours and knowing that any guest approaching the desk or contacting me by phone could be "the inspector" was exhausting and created anxiety. But since I enjoyed the natural high of juggling multiple guest requests at once, I thrived during this annual ritual. The upkeep of the hotel's facilities was not in my control, but I knew the experience I provided to guests most certainly was, and my department needed to execute to perfection signature Five Diamond moments:

- Did the doorman check for the guest's name on their luggage and proactively greet them by name?
- Did the bellman provide an escort and clearly share information about the various hotel outlets? Did they remember to show the guest how to use their heating and cooling controls?
- Did a member of the concierge team make a personalized dining recommendation before or after the opera?
- Did the bellman ask if luggage needed to be stored? Did they issue tags? Did they provide the guest with printed directions and a water bottle for their journey home?
- Did the doorman use the guest's name on departure, wish them a safe journey, and genuinely suggest they return?

Not knowing who the inspector was until they checked out was like being on a game show and left us guessing what was behind door number one. And as anxious as all this made me, I loved standing at my desk watching our team perform at such a high level. The seamless handoffs from Joe at the door to Ted at the front desk to Justin, who had a bell cart loaded and ready, and so on, could rival Olympic track stars competing for gold in a relay. I'm not sure the pace was sustainable beyond this intensely scrutinized period, but in the moment, it was intoxicating to deliver such stellar service.

As a team we tried to guess who the inspector was and would make Lucia aware right away. When we thought a potential inspector had just engaged us and asked some targeted questions (such as "What time does the fitness center open?" or "Do I need a reservation for afternoon tea?"), we would check their folio (a record of their billed charges) to see which services they had enjoyed throughout their stay up until that point. A true inspector would have charges at the restaurant and spa, would have ordered room service, and likely would have even enjoyed afternoon tea. They also used bellman services.

On my days off, with arms flailing to a Shakira song during Zumba class, I wondered if I was missing the inspection take place right then! My ego wanted me to be present, to be on shift, for both the undercover inspection and for the big reveal. The inspector checked out, settled any outstanding charges, and exited the hotel. Shortly thereafter they returned—always the same day—and asked for Mr. Benton, who was left with a copy of a detailed report he then disseminated and discussed at the weekly executive committee meeting. Lucia brought back a copy of the report and reviewed it with our department. I'd highfive colleagues that were named, knowing they helped us achieve a rating of five.

Once I was on duty when an inspector, a mild-mannered Caucasian man in a suit, presented me with his business card. I did not recognize him, but I did recognize the AAA on his card. My cheeks began to flush, but I calmly announced to the executive office via phone that a special guest was before me. A Five Diamond standard is to escort a guest when directions are requested, so I gestured for the inspector to follow me. I remember feeling self-conscious about my frumpy Mephisto Mary Janes sticking out in plain sight from underneath my poorly tailored black uniform slacks. They were flat, with rubber soles and Velcro (despite costing $300) but were necessary for my high arches and the marble underfoot. They were usually hidden behind my podium. Fortunately, the walk was short, and I'm sure the inspector was looking ahead, not at my feet. But all I wanted to do was return to my post in the lobby.

Once back at the desk, I stood there like an ice skater waiting helplessly for their score to be announced. Within minutes we knew our fate. Five Diamond, yet again!

CELEBRITY RULES

No seeking autographs. No appearing starstruck. No preferential treatment. That's what the employee handbook section on celebrities stated, anyway.

Yeah, right. This was impossibly difficult. Yet another part of being a successful Five Diamond concierge was the art of looking cool when helping the likes of Mick Jagger, Shaquille O'Neal, Mark Wahlberg, Senator John McCain, President George H. W. Bush, Paul Giamatti, Cameron Diaz, Jim Carrey, Whoopi Goldberg, Sarah McLachlan, Josh Groban, Will Smith, Jennifer Connelly, Stevie Wonder, the Gipsy Kings, and any number of other megastars that strolled through the Rittenhouse lobby.

When Dean Cain walked up to my desk, for instance, my racing heart tested my ability to look cool.

"I need a rental car to get to Princeton University," he said.

"It would be my pleasure to assist you," I said, half smirking, half terrified, with a lump in my throat. I hoped I didn't smell from my uniform being overdue to be dry-cleaned.

Dean was registered at the hotel, but most celebrities, I learned quickly, used a fictitious name. During my teen years, I loved following him as dreamy Clark Kent in *Lois & Clark: The New Adventures of Superman.*

I handed him a pen and asked him to take a few minutes to fill out the form, and I let him know I'd need his driver's license number and credit card. After he handed them to me, I discovered he was older than I thought. I walked into the back office to copy them and said, "Look what I've got!" and showed off his license to my colleagues before returning to the concierge desk. I wanted to be his personal escort to Princeton and show him the back roads to get there. Since my college was right around the corner, I would have been a perfect tour guide. But of course I couldn't say any of that and watched him walk out the front door.

When murmurings of a Rolling Stones visit erupted, I never expected to see Mick Jagger himself. He arrived late one night postshow, using the back door to avoid autograph seekers congregating out front. I was standing at the desk when I saw him from the neck up, his bangs fluffy. A security detail surrounded him and soon whisked him out a secret exit.

NBA teams used the main entrance and arrived via tour bus. They paraded past my desk—fifteen men in matching warm-ups. On television Shaquille O'Neal, who at the time was playing for the Miami Heat, seemed to tower over his teammates and the other opponents, which is striking since everyone in the NBA is considered tall. But when I looked up from making a reservation at Deux Cheminées and saw seven-foot-one Shaq about three feet from my desk as he joked with another teammate (who was only six five), I felt like I was looking up at a NYC sky-scraper. Yes, he was taller than I'd ever imagined him to be. A giant of a human. I smiled, waved, and said, "Welcome!"

Most of my interactions with celebrities came by way of their tour manager, who often reached out to us by phone long before they were scheduled to arrive. For instance, Mark Wahlberg was a guest for nearly a three-month stretch while filming *Invincible*, a sports drama based on the true story of Vince Papale, who played for the Philadelphia Eagles from 1976 to 1978. Mark's manager approached us at the concierge desk almost daily to schedule golf tee times on his days off or to ask for food delivery recommendations. I often wanted to ask if Mark had any other hobbies, but it was also exciting to be indirectly helping a celebrity.

The keep-it-cool test was especially challenging when Cameron Diaz was on-site for a month during the filming of *In Her Shoes*, a chick flick set in Rittenhouse Square. When she strolled by, her toothy smile, dimples, and everything else you see in the movies was there. She was perfect. I'd read Jennifer Weiner's book of the same name when it came out in 2002, with my toes buried in the sand. I'd been thrilled to hear it was going to be adapted into a Hollywood film and ecstatic to learn it was filming in Philadelphia.

The next month Whoopi Goldberg called down to the desk, and I answered. She said she wanted a Caesar salad from Lacroix with not one but two parmesan twills.

"I love twills too," I said. "My pleasure."

And then there was Jim Carrey, my favorite comedic actor from the nineties, who appeared at the hotel in an oversize jacket and baseball hat. He had requested before arrival that a treadmill be placed in his room, facing east—in my experience, a bizarre, or at least unusual, request. He passed by the concierge desk silently and walked toward the exit, looking down, which left me with a sense of disappointment.

Philadelphia's hosting of Live 8, a concert that sought to raise money to fight poverty and disease in Africa, was the pinnacle of celebrity sightings at the Rittenhouse. The free concert would last over eight hours, and nonorganizers estimated a crowd size that topped one million.

Many of the performers stayed with us. Who would get the presidential suite?

Nobody in the front office wanted to be responsible for making any of the stars feel like they were less important than another. The lobby became a scene you'd only expect to see on the Oscars red carpet. Our security team, outfitted in dark suits and headsets, were positioned strategically to support the individual entourages. The elevator bank was in constant motion, full of hairdressers, makeup artists, personal assistants, talent managers, and celebrities headed to and from the Benjamin Franklin Parkway. I stood at my desk, smiling and nodding, amazed I had a front-row seat to it all.

In the days leading up to the big concert, I somehow found a way to keep picking up my jaw each time a celebrity would walk or stand nearby. Like when Josh Groban and Sarah McLachlan debriefed about their upcoming collaboration on her hit song "Angel" a mere foot from my desk. Josh's hair was extra shaggy, which became his signature style, and I laughed out loud when his tour manager approached later that day about a haircut appointment.

Will Smith, Stevie Wonder, Jennifer Connelly, and

many others slept overnight at the Rittenhouse for the week. My workplace quite literally became a revolving door of exceptional talent performing or presenting at the live benefit concert. Assisting those with the star power to raise hundreds of millions of dollars for such a worthwhile cause filled me with an overwhelming sense of pride.

A sense of joy too. Helping celebrities and their staff navigate mundane tasks—food procurement, transportation, personal hygiene, recreation—reminded me that we were all just people with the same basic needs, no matter how famous.

I thought that, over time, the novelty of interacting with celebrities might wear off or the added pressure of ensuring a VIP was well taken care of might prove too intense. It did not. It was a privilege. And boasting to my friends and family was really fun.

THE GRASS IS GREENER

As both a longtime sports fan and someone keen on getting to know my colleagues even better, I sniffed around town and discovered a hotel softball league in which the Rittenhouse had never participated.

"Heck, I'm starting a team!" I told everyone.

I wanted to get out of the lobby in the gorgeous weather and was ready to lace up my cleats again. I hadn't picked up my glove since walking out of Coach Miller's office at the end of my sophomore year of college. With HR's permission I sent out a mass email to fill the squad, and by the time our first practice rolled around, we had the makings of a great team:

- Jon, from minibar, nineteen, an all-American kid, literally
- Darnell, from banquets, always carrying his balled-up tuxedo

- Dan, from accounting, in sweatpants from the seventies
- Chet, from security, with a Babe Ruth–like swing
- Lisa, from the executive office, with snacks and a medicine kit
- Omar and Steve, servers from Lacroix, best friends and polar opposites in build
- Whitney, our reservationist and necessary second female starter

But it was Eric from room service who I longed to have a catch with, especially after my recent breakup with Derrick.

When he showed up for practice and I saw for the first time that he had an athletic, trim build and sandy-blond hair, I said, "Oh my God, *you're* Eric from room service!?"

We had only ever spoken by phone. Eric worked the a.m. shift, like I often did. And when guests called to place their breakfast orders, he took them. On busy mornings, when a guest couldn't get through to room service, our hotel operator, Rose, patched the call through to me, and I took the order or acknowledged that their tray was ready to be picked up. I then called Eric. In a Five Diamond setting, someone always picks up the phone. There is no option for voicemail. If I was confirming an in-room amenity, like wine, for a VIP guest, or ordering chocolate-covered strawberries, I needed to speak with Eric.

Although we talked constantly at work, it was his major-league range at shortstop—scooping up balls left, right, forward, back—that caught my eye. Eric also had a laid-back charm and an eff-you attitude to authority and rules, something that, in my mid-twenties, made me giggle and flip my hair.

Had he wondered what I looked like as well, all these months?

Led by Eric's mastery, our young squad—decked out in ringer T-shirts, white with black trim and designed by Tim at the front desk—had the grit of the reigning World Series champs. Immediately we started winning games. Teammates passed through the lobby recounting and laughing about the highlights from the night before. In the break room, our team formed a lunch-table clique. Even Mr. Benton lingered by my desk for a second or two longer to congratulate me on the team's performance.

It was my first experience with team building (outside of a happy hour), and I simply loved interacting with people! I loved hearing about what happened in some of the departments I wasn't familiar with, like minibar (replenishing condoms, lube, and scotch), and came to appreciate their small but important role on the team. My crush on Eric and my participation on the team lightened the intensity of work and being stuck in the lobby. Having a softball game to look forward to midweek made clocking sixteen hours each weekend easier.

When the season came to an end, so did my fling with Eric. And I no longer looked forward to ordering chocolate strawberries for a guest.

REVOLVING DOOR

Standing in the lobby during yet another loud, drunken wedding, I rolled my eyes and told my coworker Alicia, "Let's go out tonight! How about Continental Midtown?" I was single and I wanted to have a little fun. Alicia was single too—and fearless and fun and frequently my accomplice.

At the bar, waiting three people deep to order a drink, I saw a dark-haired guy in jeans and a button-down shirt flash a smile at me. His friend did as well. They paid for our Pimm's cups and asked us to join them. The rest of the night, we sat together and talked about what it was like working at a luxury hotel.

I learned that Rich was in town from Washington, DC, for the weekend and was staying with his buddy Pete, who lived nearby. They were former coworkers at the Environmental Protection Agency. Conversation was easy, drinks were flowing, and at the end of the night, I let Rich walk me home.

I lived in a studio apartment in a sixteen-story building with a doorman, high ceilings, built-in bookshelves, and twenty-seven layers of paint, just a block from Rittenhouse Square. I knew there were security cameras outside, and Willy the doorman always looked out for me.

I had a 7:00 a.m. shift the next morning but didn't want the night to end. Inhaling the aroma of the late-night pizza baking across the street, I felt a pit in my stomach when Rich kissed me good night but didn't ask for my number. I fell asleep dreaming of being the girlfriend of a corporate attorney scheduled to take Amtrak back to DC in the morning.

The next morning, while storing luggage, I thought, *I don't want to work weekends anymore.* An hour later, knee deep in checkouts, Shamus, the doorman, stood in front of my podium—with him, my handsome attorney, Rich!

He smirked. "Hello again! I'd like to get your number."

I felt my eyes widen, heart beat faster, face burn. I was floored. Flattered. Beet red. I glanced over at Alicia, who was in the middle of a checkout, and she kept on keeping on. During our escapades the night before, Alicia and I had mentioned where we worked, and he hadn't forgotten.

That moment led to a year and a half of long-distance dating, but Rich wasn't willing to move back to Philly, and I wasn't willing to move to DC. Though heartbroken, I learned two important things.

One: I wanted to find a husband.

Two: If you work at a hotel, beware of who you tell!

The following weekend, there I stood yet again, in the smoke, staring at another bride and groom, wondering how I would get out.

SUPER BOWL SUNDAY

When the Philadelphia Eagles returned to the Super Bowl for the first time in more than twenty years, I wanted to watch the game in my sweatpants with my family more than anything in the world. And to watch it just like old times: in "the new room" (our living room), eating Mom's multilevel taco dip, and sipping a Swiss Farms tea cooler.

Four days before the big game, I arrived at work to see my name written on the schedule on the very day of the Super Bowl. I composed myself. The prior year I had attended every single Eagles home game as a press box runner. I was not a fair-weather fan. I bled green. While working for the media-relations team, I refilled journalists' water bottles and handed out postgame quotes for stories. My favorite moment was standing beside future Hall of Fame quarterback Tom Brady in the postgame interview room, collecting his quotes for distribution.

Now, with the least amount of seniority, I'd be stuck behind the concierge desk during the biggest moment in Philadelphia sports history since I was born. I hoped one of my colleagues would volunteer to take my shift. But when no one did, I welled up with tears, especially because I knew some of them didn't care about the actual game of football but were interested only in the spectacle of commercials and a halftime performance by Paul McCartney.

I called my dad and told him I had to work and was upset. Really upset.

He understood and tried to comfort me. If anyone could understand the devastation I felt, and the anticipation of the Eagles bringing home a championship, it was him.

The day of the game, thirty feet from where I stood at my desk, cheers and boos erupted from within Smith & Wollensky as diehard Eagles fans took in every play. But I could only listen to the emotive bursts and wager a guess on what had just happened. A touchdown? An important first down? An interception? A timely penalty flag?

I was depressed and isolated, with just Rosella near me at the front desk. Nobody was checking in. Nobody was walking through the lobby. Everybody was glued to their television. Everyone except me. I didn't have a single guest request all night—just a few people passing through, commenting, "Oh, I'm really sorry you are stuck working."

Streaming the game from the concierge desk or my flip phone was, of course, impossible in those days. The best I could do was continuously refresh the box score on my desk computer after each cheer and boo.

Rosella, who hated football, paced behind the front desk to keep busy. I matched her. Rosella said things like "Do you think the Patriots are still ahead?" or "Tom Brady is just so good!" And all I wanted to do was wallow in self-pity.

"Rosella, I just don't know," I snapped.

Win or lose, I wasn't in control of my schedule and would never be if I stayed at this job. I stood in the vastness of the marble lobby, its own lifeless enclave. I had never felt so disconnected from the city I loved. The Birds lost to the Patriots, 21–24.

The next day everyone asked me, "Hey, did you see the play?" and "Hey, did you see that commercial?"

No. No, I did not.

OCCUPANCY

UPWARD TRAJECTORY

Detached and disenchanted, I began to update my résumé after the Super Bowl, but I still continued going through the motions each day for more than a year.

On Fourth of July weekend 2006, I stepped out the back entrance in jean shorts, smelling garbage yet again. Another wasted summer weekend. I couldn't shake the feeling that I was missing out on life. My scheduled work hours were never the same week to week, and I never had weekends off. I imagined my friend Cindy saying, "Jamie must be working again."

Cindy and my local high school friends, who worked traditional Monday through Friday jobs, mostly as teachers, stopped inviting me to things. My friend Julie moved to Colorado, and my best friend Karen moved to England to follow her Finnish boyfriend while he secured an international shipping degree. I had never worked up the guts to ask Frank for time off to visit either of them or found the time to get a passport. I'd been missing out for over two years, being on my feet all day and inhaling secondhand smoke. I'd finally had enough.

Day in and day out I began to scour the internet, Monster.com, and Hcareers for opportunities. I knew I wanted to stay in the world of luxury hospitality. It suited me, and it was also nearly impossible to go backward after working for an upscale brand.

I wanted to replicate the level of discernment and service I'd grown accustomed to and was groomed to provide for a clientele that enjoyed limousines, bottle service, and acclaimed chefs—all of which I'd enjoyed learning about, test driving, and enhancing my own life with. Everything looked so glamorous, especially when you were seeing only a small snapshot of the guest's actual life while they vacationed. I wanted to be a jet-setter too. I yearned to find a successful attorney or notable doctor to be my life partner and travel companion and have someone put rose petals on our bed.

After a summer of fruitless job searching, one fall day I read that a lead concierge position was available at a new luxury residential high-rise a few blocks from the Rittenhouse.

I emailed someone named Kayla right away.

The day of the interview, I looked up at the massive skyscraper and thought, *I hope this is a fresh start.* I walked inside and stepped into the fastest elevator ever, and I got off at fifty-seven, the top floor. I was shocked by the beauty of the eastern-facing views, the Society Hill Towers, and the sun glistening off the Delaware River.

My enchantment was interrupted when a very big man with a wrinkled, untucked shirt greeted me with a goofy grin and high-pitched *"Jaaaaamieeee!"*

The man was Richard Oller, Kayla's boss. And unlike David Benton, with his reserved demeanor and unreadable face, Richard smiled, patted my shoulder, and said, "Welcome to the Residences at Two Liberty Place! What do you think?"

With Richard's aura and his welcoming vibe, I already knew I'd fit in well. But I calmly said, "I can't believe people will be lucky enough to live here."

"And work here," he replied.

Richard and I made our way to a living-room environment and settled in.

"Let me tell you about the lifestyle we are trying to create," he began. "The thirty-seventh floor up to the fifty-seventh is under construction, and it will be residential. We need someone to lead a team tasked with creating white-glove services for the residents moving in. We want you to be the person to make it happen."

"Great," I said, rolling my shoulders back—while in disbelief about how quickly he'd offered me the role.

He winked. "When can you start?"

I played it cool and said I'd need the weekend to mull things over, but as I descended in the elevator, I was already contemplating what I'd wear on my first day.

Two weeks later, in January 2007, nearly three years after I'd first stepped foot in the Rittenhouse, I found a new home in hospitality. On my first day at Two Liberty Place, I arrived on the fifty-seventh floor and asked about my desk's whereabouts.

"What desk?" Richard said. "Here's my Staples card."

Soon afterward, I sat at my newly purchased desk with a cell phone and a hard hat nearby. Each day, when we walked the raw spaces on the lower floors in various states of construction—concrete floor, pillars, glass windows, conceptualizing and measuring amenities, dust everywhere—I realized the uniqueness of getting to transform something from nothing.

Preparing for the residents' move-in was a thrill. Richard expected the Residences at Two Liberty Place to have the best service in all of Philadelphia. I wanted that too. Along with the newly hired general manager, Alex Cohen, we got to work.

We had to take the sterile footprint of these newly constructed rooms—business center, lounge, media room, fitness studio, pool, locker rooms, and more—and create vibrancy and function. Which chairs would be most comfortable in the business center? How did we want to configure the package-storage room? Would the massage rooms have a towel warmer? Our number one priority was to make residents feel at home. To be comfortable. To want for nothing.

To bring these rooms to life, we had to think and act like a guest. I took home sample bath amenities, slippers, robes, and towels, each procured from different wholesale providers, to see which felt the most luxurious, were within budget, and had wide appeal to both male and female residents. For a few weeks, I pampered myself, trying out different lines of Gilchrist & Soames, L'Occitane, and Kiehl's body washes, shampoos, and hand soaps. After calling the Four Seasons, the Rittenhouse, and Toppers Spa to discover which brand of robes they carried, I tested out samples.

"What did you think of the lavender scent?" Alex asked one morning.

"Not unisex enough," I said.

The next morning: "Did you like how your skin felt after?"

"Yes. Very refreshing."

"Was the robe too heavy? Or just right?"

"It was too expensive for the weight. Let's try the brand the Four Seasons recommended."

I ended up choosing everything: Matching chrome hand pumps with liquid hand soap and lotion flanked each sink. Each locker room shower stall had a wall-mounted dispenser of body wash, shampoo, and conditioner. The sound system played classical music I selected. Marble floors were buffed with pads I purchased. Lit sconces lined the hallways with bulbs I tested.

I sat at my desk, wrapped with marble counters on three out of four sides, and played barista, offering espresso from our expensive machine to welcome prospective buyers and new residents to the club floor.

My grandmother's congratulatory gift—a snow globe of Philadelphia that showcased tourist highlights—sat perched on the front of my desk. Everyone who entered the floor saw it. We were ready to welcome people home.

INTRODUCTIONS

Richard announced to the sales team and myself that I'd be available to help and provide concierge services to owners before they were even ready to move in. I sat at my desk, ready for my residential debut and wanting to make a great first impression.

Over the phone and in person, I listened to what every resident needed: "Jamie, would you be able to get my car inspected?" or "Jamie, can you give keys to my house-keeper?" or "Jamie, can you sign for a sofa delivery?"

Yes, yes, yes! I was their go-to gal, and I fulfilled each request with a smile.

An in-house sales team of three dynamic real estate agents met and toured prospective buyers through model units and explained the amenities found on the club floor. Instead of handing buyers brochures promising concierge services, I made sure to be at my actual desk. I'd reach out my hand to introduce myself and say, "Good morning! I look forward to being your personal assistant."

Once a resident was under contract on a unit, I called to schedule an "owner interview"—a custom intake session

designed to explain the services we offered at the concierge desk and to become familiar with their interests and
plans for using their new home. I also used the meeting to
gift and wow them with a custom Philadelphia snow globe,
similar to the one my grandmother had given me. Within
the little glass ball, snow fell on One and Two Liberty
Place, city hall, the Betsy Ross House, Pat's King of Steaks
and Geno's Steaks, the Liberty Bell, and the Philadelphia
Museum of Art, all while a lullaby of the *Rocky* theme song
played.

I started each interview with basic questions and
branched out based on the resident's level of engagement
and personality:

- Was Two Liberty their full-time residence, or
  do they own another home as well?
- Whom do they expect to be frequent visitors?
- Do they have a pet?
- What car(s) do they drive?

I loved learning which sports teams they rooted for,
their favorite bands, the alcoholic drinks they enjoyed,
where they liked to eat on a Saturday night, and their most
memorable travel destination. I felt like my childhood hero
Bob Costas, expertly interviewing my subject, making
sure each question led with a who, what, where, when, or
why. Some interviews lasted upward of two hours and usually translated into a future resident who regularly used
our services. I learned quickly that even the most demanding resident wasn't going to check out like a guest at the
Rittenhouse.

After each interview I typed up the findings and

distributed them to Alex and the future concierge team. No corporate speak or manual. I created files for each resident for the benefit of the team. Having an advance, in-depth look at who they were allowed us to immediately provide those white-glove services Richard had insisted upon from the beginning.

For Ms. Leonard, I recommended a housekeeper. For the Klemmes, who lived full-time in California, I facilitated some home improvement estimates. For the Montufars, I secured dinner reservations at my favorite place, the American gem called Friday Saturday Sunday, because they said they were up for a new adventure.

Though not a single resident yet lived in the building, and wouldn't for months, I hoped my outreach proved my value as the go-to gal. Serving residents was eye opening. How easy and addicting it was to provide a personalized recommendation based on an established rapport and intimate understanding of their interests or needs. I became truly invested in the joy of helping them. For example, I knew Dr. Dormans collected Southwestern antiques (pottery, Aztec urns, quilts, pillows, etc.) and was mulling over the idea of creating some custom built-ins in his den to properly showcase his treasures. Simultaneously, I knew Mr. and Mrs. Knox had just hired a lovely custom woodworker, and with both parties' permission, I was able to make the introduction.

Each day I felt needed. Residents were asking for me. I was busy and earnestly becoming like Frank, my first mentor and lead concierge at the Rittenhouse. But I was making the role my own, trading Frank's air kisses for my serious tasking. I wasn't a natural schmoozer. I was a constant email sender, phone-call answerer, research finder, and persistent to-do lister.

Our residents expected this high level of service, and we made sure the inaugural team was up for the challenge. I wanted to find the right people the first time around, despite having no recruiting experience. Alex and I sat in a windowless room, creating a staffing plan, writing up job descriptions, posting job ads, and prescreening candidates. Sorting through hundreds of résumés, some of them hand delivered, without a dedicated human resources team was a monumental task.

I had never looked at a résumé other than my own, so I only knew how to be the interviewee. But I couldn't let our candidates know that. I didn't want Alex to know, either, lest he assign me a different task. I decided to research popular interview questions and fake it till I made it.

Together, we focused first on the big picture and talked through the ebb and flow of a day at Two Liberty Place. We looked at each shift and day of the week and decided the number of staff members needed. And we thought about where it made sense to outsource instead, like for valet and housekeeping. My task felt daunting: I needed to forecast residential demand and occupancy in a building still being built. We couldn't skimp on employees if we wanted to be the best residence in the city.

For the concierge desk, I needed to hire three additional people—one full-time and two part-time—since our desk would be open seven days a week from 7:00 a.m. to 11:00 p.m. To narrow the field, we conducted interviews with only those who had served previously as a concierge, worked at a hotel, or had experience with luxury clientele.

Charles, a former Ritz-Carlton concierge, was our unanimous selection for the full-time evening position. Sharon, who had also previously been a hotel concierge, most recently at the Loews, was hired as a weekend part-timer, and Albert, who had been a front desk agent at a nearby upscale hotel, rounded out the team. On paper it was a dream team, full of hospitality veterans comfortable serving individuals with high expectations.

In reality, I hadn't spoken to Charles's, Sharon's, and Albert's respective employers to vet them, and once they were hired, I found myself carrying much of the workload because of their lack of comfort using the computer. I hadn't realized there was a huge difference in skill set between making a single dinner reservation, especially when the restaurant is specifically requested, and a larger, more complex request like creating a weekend itinerary without firsthand experience. One is a transaction and can be replaced by an iPad; the other takes initiative and detailed research and often a back-and-forth conversation with the resident.

Unfortunately, I'd unknowingly hired a team of schmoozers, and I was frequently left being the primary doer. Mrs. Hernandez liked to talk with Charles about her new nail color, but she came to me to find out where to have her vehicle inspected. So did Mr. Dizer and Ms. Slattery. My veteran squad shied away from maintaining a spreadsheet, booking a flight with points, and complex event planning. Some residents would simply wait for my shift if they had a complex request. I likely enabled this behavior as well, since it was easier for me to tackle additional work than it was to spend hours helping everyone else play catch-up.

Charles started calling out with more regularity and sometimes with no communication at all. Albert amassed a bunch of callouts too. Meanwhile, Sharon, who was coachable and reliable, was promoted to full-time. And as a more seasoned recruiter this time around, I needed to find someone who was comfortable being uncomfortable and who would continuously push me to be better.

Because of a personal referral, I took a chance and interviewed Alexa. I thought back to Jeffrey and what he had done for me, landing me my big break at the Rittenhouse. Otherwise, I would have passed over Alexa, a twenty-four-year-old bubbly brunette. No, she hadn't held the title of concierge before. Nor had she worked at an upscale hotel. In fact, she hadn't worked at any hotel. She had spent her brief professional career as an account manager for a notable Philadelphia public relations firm. All in all, a situation not unlike the one in which I had found myself when Lucia, the Rittenhouse's front-office manager, took a chance on me.

My gamble on Alexa paid off. No matter what I asked of her—"Alexa, can you research newly opened restaurants?" or "Alexa, can you put together a draft of our Weekend Top Ten List?"—the answer was almost always a version of "Yes!" or "You bet. I'm eager to try it."

Not once did I hear, "Well, we used to do it like this." (Because she hadn't done it before!)

She efficiently logged packages, scheduled house-car reservations, and found ways to be productive during down time. I knew I could delegate a task to her, even without a deadline, and it would get done swiftly and correctly.

Hiring Alexa not only made our concierge department better, but it made me better too. I longed for a new challenge, to grow and to be able to provide dynamic offerings beyond my own personal set of experiences. Hiring a star player like Alexa was an opportunity to free myself from the desk for a few hours each day to focus on engaging the team and enhancing our work culture, two areas becoming near and dear to me. Now I could simply say, "Thank you, Alexa!" and walk to the back office to prep for a new-hire orientation.

CREATING THE BEST LIFESTYLE EVER

"I need you to find out what the condo fees are around the city," Richard Oller said one day. He wanted to know how we compared to our competitors. But I was more interested to know what lifestyle the fee afforded.

Desk staff at condos around the city serve a security function, but if you asked for a restaurant recommendation, you'd be handed the phone book. As other Center City condominiums began using the term *concierge* for their desk staff, mostly as a marketing gimmick, I wanted to make sure Two Liberty's reputation was in another league. I wanted residents to brag to friends and loved ones.

This meant snuffing out the competition. Undercover. I was a journalist again.

A tax abatement program passed in 2000 incentivized developers in Philadelphia to build new condominiums or repurpose existing structures and convert them. As a result, between 2007 and 2009, over twelve new condominium buildings broke ground and opened in Center City, the main downtown corridor situated between the Schuylkill and Delaware Rivers. All were boasting concierge services.

I enlisted the help of my dad's dental colleague Maria, who was middle aged and conveniently looking to buy a home. She would be the perfect person to help me with my ruse. She was the homebuyer; I was her friend tagging along for support. I made us numerous appointments with sales associates so we could be shown actual units in addition to the amenities found within each community. Some of the appointments were at sales centers because the infrastructure of the future residential high-rise was not yet complete. Maria, who is a vivacious and fun person by nature, was an eager accomplice. We set off during the middle of my workday, and that, in itself, was super cool. It felt like I was starring in my own episode of *House Hunters* and getting paid for it.

Each condominium had its own flavor, and many even had advantages over Two Liberty—by way of location, lesser condo fee, wine storage, ability to self-park in a deeded parking spot, and so on. I snooped around trying to ascertain the level of service provided at the concierge desk:

- I chatted with the on-duty concierge, asking about things they most commonly helped residents with, knowing that the answer would likely be package storage and distribution.
- I asked them if they had a business card, as this simple piece of paper was an indicator as to whether they had a relationship with the

outside business community. It would also tell me if they had an email address.

- I peered over their desk, looking for a computer, to see if they communicated with residents in ways other than by phone. Were they still using an old-fashioned clipboard or notebook, or did they use property management software to log visitors, key sign-outs, and packages?

- I found out which hours the concierge desk was staffed and if there was a separate concierge in addition to the doorman or porter. Without redundancy the concierge is often expected to serve as a laborer.

- I asked if the concierge had previously worked in a hotel setting in some capacity and if they had an affiliation with the Philadelphia Area Concierge Association.

I became fascinated with the sliding scale of service found within each individual community, and I created a rating system for concierge desks so that prospective residents had a sense of what was really being offered. As I suspected, developers frequently misused the word *concierge* in their marketing materials and purposely included phrases like *on duty 24/7, white glove*, and *hotel style*, when I knew that in most cases, the on-duty concierge was a kind but resourceless security guard, lacking a necessary lifeline to the pulse of the city. Now I had proof.

I proudly presented Richard with my spreadsheet, inclusive of pricing per square foot, monthly condo fees, inclusion or omission of utilities, and the on-site amenities. I loved assessing the competition, and it made me feel proud and even more excited about what we were planning to offer at Two Liberty.

The expectations were high, and I was in the driver's seat.

THE KEYS

Alex handed me the keys to the locked uniform closet. "I need your help filling this."

I felt the keys in my hand and bit my lower lip. Alex, who had a degenerative eye condition, pointed to the empty closet and said, "Make sure everyone looks good."

"Okay," I said—and immediately called Boyds, who'd outfitted me years ago at the Rittenhouse.

My goal was to pick out the perfect uniform for the entire staff and hand a full garment bag of new uniform pieces to each member of our inaugural team.

First, I admired and selected a modern charcoal gray suit. That took only a few minutes. But which tie felt on brand with a luxury high-rise community? Hmm. The tie needed to feel expensive but not actually be expensive. It needed to make a statement from a distance, hide stains up close, complement the lobby and our logo.

In the end I selected a two-tone diagonal-stripe blue tie. It complemented the cool tones of the lobby and the light-blue collared blouses with subtle gray lines of the uniform that Sharon, Alexa, and I wore. I wanted the staff to own it and feel good in their uniforms. I wanted residents and visitors to our community to have the initial impression of "Wow, they look sharp!" I wanted the same to be true for our housekeepers and maintenance staff, in their embroidered polo shirts and khakis. My hope was that when we all had our "costumes" on, we would stand up a little straighter, smile a little wider, and be ready to tackle anything thrown our way.

Once all the uniform pieces were delivered, including custom doormen hats, I placed each individual garment bag inside the closet. Then I called everyone separately to the club floor to help them get dressed. Suddenly I felt like I was in retail. But I had never worked in retail. Some of the men were petite. Some were built like bouncers.

Just when I'd thought I was done, Anthony, a doorman, unexpectedly gave his notice. He handed me a ball of smelly doorman clothes—the uniform's return was a requirement to receive a final paycheck—and I rolled my eyes and said thanks. I sent them to the dry cleaner, and not for the last time: turnover remained high in customer-facing roles. Employees also grew and shrunk. I learned it was an endless task.

Since uniform distribution was my ongoing responsibility, I had to be keenly organized: small to large, left to right, dress shirts, vests, overcoats, raincoats, suit jackets, suit pants. There was no turning back. I loved having the keys and felt like a real manager.

Timiko, who I'd recruited from the Rittenhouse, asked me one day, "Do you have another tie?"

"Where are the three I gave you?"

Timiko shrugged.

So I became the uniform police.

I also became well versed in which men's sizes were most common (42R) and could correctly identify which new hires needed extra length to ensure their suit jacket covered their rear end. In the closet I'd find suitable garments for each of my newest colleagues and pray that what I had in stock was still in good condition and would fit. Or I'd stall a few days, asking them to wear ill-fitting clothes, until I could have them appropriately sized at Boyds. It was a delicate balance between not wanting to invest thousands of dollars on new seasonal uniform pieces and ensuring a staff member had what they needed to look the part during their ninety-day introductory period. And I learned a number of things I never expected in the process:

- Men's shirts came in two sizes, and you needed to determine both the neck and sleeve size for proper fit. For example, an overweight man could have a wide neck but short arms.
- My coworkers wore through the groin of their pants.
- "Ring around the collar" was real. Collars easily developed a dark-yellow stain.
- My colleagues needed multiple reminders to switch out their shirts, use collar stays, and be mindful of weight gain. Extra-large sizes cost more, and we didn't have many in stock. If a coworker gained weight, we could let out their pants only so much.
- The men's locker room smelled badly of body odor and dirty socks. I pinched my nose every time I retrieved former employees' balled-up

uniforms from the bottom of a peach-colored locker.

- We went through white gloves with incredible speed. When Two Liberty Place officially opened, we had two hundred pairs. Each employee got ten pairs. I told everyone to handle them with care. In reality, the gloves ended up rumpled and stained, and when Ellis laundered them with bleach, they shrunk down to the hand size of a ten-year-old. A shrunken grayish-white glove wasn't so magical.

Yet I loved wearing a uniform: the ease of getting dressed in the morning and the great privilege of representing a luxury brand. To me, a doorman in full regalia positioned in front of a building, holding open the door with a smile on their face is a universal sign of distinction. It is also a way to create uniformity among employees of diverse backgrounds. Several employees didn't own suits, and I loved how uniforms gave us all an opportunity to strip away the personal and serve while being somebody else in the workplace.

Unlike at the Rittenhouse, I was the only one policing uniform standards. When staff became lax, their name tags went missing, doorman hats were "borrowed" by team members across different shifts, and the white gloves became just a marketing cliché. Even though our staff were proud to suit up on day one, by day ten the novelty of the head-to-toe ensemble had worn off. And correcting it required tireless nagging and sometimes even a complaint by a resident: "Who is that new employee? He's not even wearing a proper uniform!"

New employees were quick to slip when they realized that their counterparts—and worse yet, their shift supervisor—weren't suited up properly. The summer months consistently had the worst compliance. While I sat inside in the luxury of air conditioning, helping residents, I felt for a team dripping with sweat, baking on the hot asphalt in their full suit. And, like me at the Rittenhouse, probably wondering about their next career move.

I jostled the keys in my pocket, wondering who was going to give notice next.

A PRIVILEGE

A year into my job, I noticed that I was everybody's first stop, not just for tasks but to share news.

For instance, Barbara, a baby boomer resident who could have been my mother, once stopped by to unload a suite of personal concerns: "We are going to dinner this weekend, and I still don't know what to wear," she said. "And I work out five days a week, and I still don't like how my clothes fit me, and I haven't seen my grandkids in a month. . . ."

I nodded along, unable to relate.

Then Mary, a retiree with too much time on her hands, stopped by to whisper, "Did you hear who is moving in? Are they really married?"

I say yes, not sure why Mary cares.

Then an older couple, the DiLibertos, asked over the phone, "Can you hold our mail? Tom's having a knee replacement, and we won't be back for a while."

I say yes. I could take care of that for them.

I was becoming intimately intertwined in their lives. I suddenly had a front-row seat, a rare glimpse into private milestones, and it was a privilege. But the deeper I got into my Two Liberty Place tenure, the more unpredictable things occurred, things not in my job description: I experienced the first death, the first baby being born, and the first breakup unfolding.

DEATH

In March 2009, I never expected to be sitting at my desk ordering more staff uniforms and suddenly receive a call from the loading dock that a hospice bed was being delivered to the fortieth floor.

Since we were a small community of about fifty occupied homes on the upper floors, the absence was noticeable when a resident moved out or died. And it was especially hard when we didn't get to say goodbye. Two residents who lived alone passed away quickly from cancer diagnoses a little over a year apart. I wouldn't call myself highly emotional, but it was nevertheless a shock to see the team shed tears.

I got to know the extended families who had suffered great loss, helping facilitate funeral arrangements, furniture removal, and real estate agent access. For instance, the brother of one of our first residents to move in (Mort) called me and said, "The shiva is later today. You can send people up without calling first."

I educated the team on shiva, the Jewish ritual of family and friends coming together to tell stories about the deceased. I told them what a ripped black ribbon signified, earmarked for the spouse and siblings of the deceased. I explained how today was a great day for brevity and not a day for unnecessary schmoozing. That was one day they didn't roll their eyes and said thank you.

The day of the shiva, I could never have predicted how weird it was to meet Mort's brother, with tears in his eyes, for the first time. I'd never seen a man openly cry.

Heart beating, hands sweating, I said, "I'm so sorry about your brother."

Was I saying the right thing?

"Thank you," he said.

He then discussed details and plans for selling the unit.

Alex thoughtfully reserved the house car for staff members to travel north on Broad Street to Rodeph Shalom so we could pay our respects to Mort. While I sat in the domed and ornately tiled sanctuary that day, I thought to myself that this man had been a mere stranger to me less than two years prior.

A few months after the shiva, my father called and said, "Poppy has died." I was devastated to lose my grandfather. And I couldn't help but compare it to Mort's death and feel more intimately than ever before how death surrounds us.

BABIES

Twice a week, Gina, a young doctor, reserved the house car to go to 922 Pine Street. I was curious about the address. When I looked it up, I gasped. It was a prenatal wellness studio. Even though she wasn't showing, Gina was pregnant!

Keeping Gina's news secret until she was ready to share it with others was a responsibility I took seriously.

Although she didn't know that I knew, I was bursting inside and wanted to congratulate her. But I waited until she was ready to make an announcement.

Another expecting mama, who was a medical resident, relied heavily on online shopping, and large boxes arrived from Pottery Barn Kids and Babies"R"Us. We received, logged, and stored all deliveries at the concierge desk, and I found room for what I presumed to be her crib, stroller, and other baby supplies. Tasked with keeping a poker face until she was ready to divulge her secret, I said, "Sally, another large package has arrived for you. Can we bring it up?" Eventually her proud husband shared the big news.

When I first started at Two Liberty Place, no children lived in the community. We were used to grandkids visiting on weekends, but when a resident first alerted me that they were pregnant, it felt like a member of my own family was pregnant. Three couples had babies during my tenure, and I felt like a proud aunt meeting their little ones. Babies offered a lovely change of pace and lightened everyone's mood.

BREAKUPS

Breakups were the worst, because it was often our favorite half of the couple who moved out. Bachelors and divorcés made up a significant slice of our resident population, and some of these men decided to live on-site with their girlfriends. If you live in a freestanding house, nobody witnesses the drama of a breakup or a move. But in a community setting, not only is the staff aware, but all the residents are aware, too, and they are not your friends.

Finding oneself in the middle of people's sticky business was tricky. Especially since the freight elevator reservations for move-ins and move-outs passed through our concierge desk. It was super awkward when a resident came to us and said, "I broke up with so-and-so. She took the cat. Please revoke her entry privileges."

It often went like this: the male owner of the unit came to us to change his permission-to-enter forms, deactivate elevator fobs, and in some cases provide us with new house keys after a locksmith changed the locks. One time a resident gave his ex-girlfriend's fob to his new girlfriend. For weeks she swiped the elevator keypad, registering the ex-girlfriend's name, and our entire staff chuckled. I eventually told the resident what was happening, and we reassigned the fob.

Since I had a genuine rapport with these women (in some cases I liked them a whole lot more than the male owner), the goodbyes were difficult. I expressed my sympathies for the end of the relationship and coordinated the move-out to be as pain-free as possible.

Two move-outs involved divorces, and the staff was caught in the middle of a lot of big feelings. One involved split custody of a toddler. Other than saying, "How have you been?" and exchanging pleasantries with our former resident when she routinely came to pick up and drop off her daughter, there wasn't much else to say. Other residents, on the way to the mail room or the fitness center, made inquiries in passing about the split, trying to find out if the gossip was true. This became my new normal.

Our most difficult split involved Tina. She was one of the first residents to move in, in March of 2008, and her casual California-hippie vibe and long, flowing blond hair was refreshing and made her stand out in an otherwise buttoned-up community. She made bell-bottoms and tassels cool again. She was friendly and approachable, and we loved her. Tina didn't work and was home most of the time. Her husband had a high-powered job, which had prompted their relocation to Philadelphia. He made sure that everyone knew his title by flashing his business card.

After Tina lived a year or so at Two Liberty, we abruptly learned that her husband would be moving out. Tina would get to keep the condo for now. I can't remember how I came to be in the know, but Tina's loneliness had led her to the bedroom of a surgeon who lived on the floor above. He was divorced. Their relationship ended not too long after it started, and we were informed that Tina would also be moving out, to return to California.

What I couldn't have predicted was that her ex-husband (and our former resident) was going to move back in, this time with his new girlfriend, a bleached blond who wore a red lip and was curvy in all the right places. We did our best to welcome them home, but it was hard to hide our discontent about the woman who had played a role in causing a marriage to end and sending Tina packing. I also empathized with her because I couldn't imagine moving into the same condo where your boyfriend had previously lived with his ex-wife. But passing judgment didn't change the fact that we were there to serve both our favorites and the ones we'd rather never see again. I didn't get to decide who lived in our community.

All these intimate shared experiences with residents were part of the magic and heartbreak of working with the same clientele day in and day out. I found myself sitting at my desk, looking out for Beverly and worrying if she missed her routine Wednesday group yoga class. And I felt uneasy when our mailman, Reggie, alerted me that Tom and Linda's mail was piling up, when I knew they hadn't traveled to Florida that winter. I cried with Lenny when his ex took their cat. I toasted with Joe when he finally retired. And I tried not to take any of my emotions home with me once my shift was over, because tomorrow would be a new day.

Easier said than done.

PROFESSIONAL ATHLETES IN THE SKY

Besides empty nesters excited to downsize and try out city living and divorcés requiring a place to pivot, Two Liberty Place became a breeding ground for professional athletes. Like with any condo association, only a certain percentage of the units could be rented out by private owners. In the case of Two Liberty, the lease length of the tenant had to be six months or longer. The community would never allow it to become a popular Airbnb destination. A short lease in a sought-after luxury building with jaw-dropping views was a win-win for athletes, who could potentially get traded at any point, and for the developer as a marketing strategy.

The 50 South Sixteenth Street address immediately became cooler when the buzz circulated about Philadelphia athletes living inside the walls of the high-rise, where residences began on the fortieth floor. It wasn't always cool for the staff. Over the span of a few years, I helped members of three out of four of our city's professional sports teams move in and out. All were renters. All stayed one year at most.

KENDRA WILKINSON AND HANK BASKETT

Hank was a wide receiver for the Philadelphia Eagles in his rookie season and returned to the team in 2010, shortly after marrying Kendra, a former Playboy model. The entire family, including infant Hank Jr. and two dogs, Martini and Raskal, moved into Two Liberty in preparation for the upcoming Eagles season.

Our door staff were thrilled to welcome the new residents home. Some neighbors were leery, as having a professional athlete living on-site instantly changed the dynamic and the anonymity of the community.

"He's not even a lock for the team," some residents stopped by my desk to say. "She looks so unassuming," said others. "I expected more."

Some nervous homeowners suggested that having Kendra and Hank as neighbors was not in the best interest of the community. What they meant was filming *Kendra*, their reality TV show, on-site at Two Liberty Place could be disruptive. Disruptive to the staff. Disruptive to residents. Disruptive to Reggie, the mailman, who had to wait on more than one occasion to deliver the mail because of crews filming adjacent to the mail room. Occasionally an elevator would be out of service for photography-equipment transport. The gym was on display because Kendra was filmed training to get her postpartum physique back. Residents would have to sign a waiver if they wanted to work out when the filming was taking place. There would be made-for-TV fights between Hank and Kendra that would escalate in the hallway of the forty-second floor. I was occasionally bumped from behind my desk and replaced by Charles, as the producers felt he was more of a character for television.

To my great surprise, I liked Kendra. She wasn't trying to flaunt her body—she was postpartum, wearing baggy clothing, trying to get back her body and her sexy swagger. Seeing her in the gym in passing, I never understood why, for the sake of ratings, she felt the need to play a ditzy blond. As if her reputation and being Hugh Hefner's ex-girlfriend were requirements for future success.

Why can't women be both smart and beautiful? I often thought.

I was embarrassed by what she represented on her television show, the ditz. Yet in person she presented a different side. I saw defeat, a weariness, and a warmth in her eyes. I wished she'd valued those parts of herself and shared them publicly.

As predicted, Hank was cut from the Eagles mid-season and the Basketts began to pack up for Minnesota. Reserving the freight elevator was a concierge task, and we were responsible for seeing them safely to the front door. But they weren't completely out of our lives. Not yet anyway. Many months later, we watched *Kendra* episodes air from during their time at Two Liberty. It was hilarious and, shockingly, filled the community association with great pride. I learned that a nontraditional celebrity resident could be a morale boost for the team but often also brought a sigh of relief upon their departure.

COLE AND HEIDI HAMELS

Because I was a former Philadelphia Phillies ball girl during the first season at Citizens Bank Park and someone who attended the final game of the 2008 World Series victory, I felt Cole and Heidi Hamels's decision to move from West Chester and reside at Two Liberty was a big deal!

Our public relations firm understandably tried to play up this story to increase hype for and sales of the remaining units. *Philadelphia Magazine* sent an editor to "live" at Two Liberty for a few days to experience life as Cole and Heidi's neighbor firsthand. Although at times it was a three-ring circus, the couple, like Hank and Kendra, were actually real, hardworking people, even building schools in Africa.

I had a crush on Cole. He was six foot, four inches tall, dark, and handsome. He radiated San Diego cool. Cole was one of the ace starting pitchers for the Phillies. And he married Heidi—the one who took off her top on *Survivor*. He was a real-life Ken, and she was a Midwestern Barbie.

When Cole approached the concierge desk, the encounter was always brief—mostly to schedule the freight elevator for a delivery. One day he walked up to my desk and said, "Jamie, can you please let me know what I need to do to get a pool table delivered to my unit?"

"Sure," I said, giddy. "What day do you expect it? I can reserve the freight elevator."

Later that night, at home, when I turned on the game and saw Cole on the mound, I smiled because I knew he liked to play pool. I felt like an insider.

In preparation for the *Philadelphia Magazine* editor's overnight stay, I had to put the finishing touches on a baseball-game outing via trolley to and from Citizens Bank Park. While it was unfortunately not Cole's night to pitch, we still had a full trolley of twenty-five residents dressed in red, plus me and the editor, headed south on Broad Street to cheer on the Phillies.

Residents bought homes at Two Liberty to have a sense of community, to make friends. Anonymity was hard to come by, with a shared mail room and a multi-layer, twenty-four seven staff. What I loved most about my job was getting to foster and encourage that sense of community. That night, while bouncing along in the trolley on the way to the game, I was proud of the mix of residents who'd chosen to spend their money and time together on an activity I had coordinated and promoted. Young and old. Singles, divorcés, and married couples. The night was perfect. A condo-association success story.

Cole and Heidi stayed only for the season, and when it was time for them to move out, Heidi approached the desk with goody baskets, personalized for each staff member, to thank us for making their year such a success. She radiated high-pitched sweetness. The couple bought a mansion in nearby Newtown Square, and another chapter would close with their scheduled move-out.

ONLY WHEN APPROACHED

From early on in my hospitality career, I knew three cardinal rules: (1) Engage in conversation only when approached; (2) smile and nod when a resident was about ten feet away; and (3) add in a warm greeting, using the time of day (e.g., "Good morning") and address residents by name when they came within five feet.

Otherwise, speak only when spoken to.

I wanted to be viewed as warm and engaging but also as someone who respected privacy and played by the rules. I desperately wanted the residents to like me. But befriending them was out of the question. This distinction, between being friendly and being friends, is a fine line. The old saying goes that a customer is your friend until they aren't, and they will be the first one to turn on you to save face. If you have a drink with them, post about it on social media, say the wrong thing, or cross a line, they will not have your back, and you will be fired. And managers must usually side with the customer.

One day I was restocking copy paper in the business center when I saw Mr. Kelsey come off the elevator on floor thirty-seven and turn the corner to the management office. I'd never seen him up here postwork other than to get his mail.

Minutes later, he left the floor in a huff, and Alex approached my desk. "He is sick and tired of the door staff acting chummy when he arrives back home after a long day of work. He just wants to quietly retire to his residence without a pat on the back and having to answer questions about his day."

"I would too," I said as I finished up at the printer.

Fortunately, we had a back door with fob access, and Mr. Kelsey made that his primary route moving forward. It reminded me of how the celebrities at the Rittenhouse had bypassed the front door.

Other residents probed and prodded and were curious to know about my private life, asking what I did over the weekend or where I had been if I'd had an unexpected day off. Eventually it felt natural to share interests and discuss social plans with residents at the concierge desk. I saw these individuals every day, at their home, often stripped down to gym clothes and no makeup, frequently at 7:00 a.m. as they passed my desk on the way to the gym. They usually stopped to talk about kids, grandkids, shore houses, or a good book.

Kathy routinely passed by my desk. She was a North Jersey transplant, a fiery and feminine brunette with reddish-blond highlights, a perfect smile, and put-together makeup. She was married to Andy, a cardiologist at UPenn. I knew from their intake interview that she loved to talk about her grown sons and what everybody else was up to.

Kathy often began a conversation, in a hushed tone, with "Did you know?"

She was someone who dropped names and liked to get personal quickly. She was the one who told me "So-and-so is moving out." She was the one to question if our newest resident was really a professional ball player. She was the one to know before anyone else that a resident was pregnant. At first I half listened to her community gossip. But then she started asking more and more about me.

On one of the many mornings she strolled past my desk to go to the gym, I shared how I'd spent the recent Jewish High Holidays listening to the sound of the shofar at synagogue and eating my grandmother's brisket.

Soon enough, although she hadn't known my exact age or my preference for men, she had found out I was single and correctly assumed that being set up with a Jewish doctor would be desirable. Kathy was the CEO of a company that planned medical meetings (which is how she'd met Andy). Consequently, Kathy also had a network of hundreds of physicians. She asked me for a photo of myself and for permission to make an email introduction to a local cardiologist.

I blushed, but quickly hit Send on my most flattering photo. I was sun kissed in the picture, and I had actually taken the time to blow-dry my hair. I loved the picture and hoped the mysterious doctor would too. He must have, because later that week, we decided to meet for drinks at a restaurant near my house.

The next day I waited sheepishly for Kathy to walk up to my desk and ask how the date went—and if I'd thought he was cute. Which she did.

"Yup!" I said.

DEMANDING
RESIDENTS

Few residents were as kind or empathetic as Kathy. Mr. Prince is case in point.

I met Mr. Prince during his owner interview, where I learned that he was in his mid-sixties and loved to run marathons. As a divorcé with two college-age kids and an accounting firm to oversee, he wanted the million-dollar condo for the prestigious address and to be taken care of by the staff.

A month after he moved in, Mr. Prince walked by my desk with a huge stack of papers and planted himself in the business center for hours.

Doesn't this guy have Wi-Fi in his unit? I thought.

He began to spend almost every day in the business center, and residents were getting infuriated. He'd spread his paperwork all over the counter, burn through entire reams of printer paper, and generally treat the space like it was his personal office. The center only had two chairs, and he sat in one, put his papers on the other, and was on the phone constantly.

He commandeered the media room too. Apparently he didn't own a TV and so felt entitled to make it his own living room. He'd sit with his feet up on the coffee table, browsing news and sports for hours on end. He even had the audacity to make out with and grope a lady friend who was in town, right there in view of everybody, late into the evening.

Residents waxed and waned in their need for our services, but not Mr. Prince. He used us nonstop to book travel, make dinner reservations, and obtain bus schedules. He called me every day or stopped by for help, and I unofficially became his personal assistant. While this was all within the bounds of my job description and included in the residents' monthly condo fee, I wondered if he was taking advantage of me and who had taken care of him before me. I soon felt like he was monopolizing the time and service that I needed to give other residents.

What I learned about Mr. Prince was that he epitomized the phrase *work hard, play hard*. He ran frequently in out-of-town races and asked me to book his travel and lodging so often that I began to think of myself as his travel agent. I booked destinations like Christchurch, New Zealand, and Antalya, Turkey, both of which required numerous flights and an awareness of time zone differences, layovers, and hotel check-ins. This was not my area of expertise. However, I liked the challenge of keeping a detailed spreadsheet of his airline, hotel, and rental-car points as well as his six credit cards on file. He told me his desired destination and a range of acceptable dates. I referenced my spreadsheet for point balances and checked with his desired providers to get the best deal. Most other residents desired the quickest flight duration. Mr. Prince didn't mind sitting for hours with multiple flight layovers just to get a cheaper fare. With him, it was always about price.

I secretly admired Mr. Prince's convoluted travel requests because I enjoyed the challenge, like a puzzle, and it helped me learn new destinations. Sometimes his calls came at inconvenient times, like when I was in the middle of purchasing theater tickets for another resident or five minutes before my shift ended. Yet I was required and happy to play the cheap-seats, Hotwire.com concierge.

But what made my blood boil was when Mr. Prince requested a last-minute change to his itinerary. Sometimes we'd set his travel plans, and later the same day he'd call back and make changes. Sometimes it was injuries that sidelined him from a race last minute, or he'd invite a lady friend—or if there had been a fight, uninvite the lady friend. These changes meant calling, canceling, updating the spreadsheet, and rescheduling. When booking with points, cancellations required endless phone calls to airlines, hotels, and other vendors to make sure account balances and credits were kosher.

One day I almost lost my cool when Mr. Prince traveled to Manhattan on the eleven-dollar Megabus, his preferred route. He asked me to make a last-minute, same-day booking for him, and I scrambled to get him one of the remaining seats. But he wasn't answering his cell phone when I needed to present two departure options. Then, in NYC, he called from a loud restaurant and asked for the return bus schedule. I was his smartphone, handler, and round-the-clock secretary, and my patience was wearing thin.

Eventually I got very tired of being Mr. Prince's

concierge, travel agent, and secretary. Though he was always complimentary and appreciative of my hard work,
he never tipped at the end of the year—except once, when
he gave me forty dollars balled up in a mug with some
Hershey's kisses. The day he handed me that mug, I knew I
wanted to be in control of my time, choose my own tasks,
and not be at the beck and call of a man who needed his
hand held.

Then there was Mrs. Calhoun, an opinionated middle-
aged woman with a thick Irish accent. She worked out at
the on-site gym and once strolled back to my desk to say,
"There are hair clumps in the shower drains!" She was
still in her sweaty workout clothes, and I knew she hadn't
showered.

Week after week it was always a new complaint.

"Thanks for letting us know, Mrs. Calhoun," I'd say yet
again, wishing she'd just move out. "We're on it."

But one weekend when I was off, she stopped by the
desk and booked the house car for her daughter's graduation from Temple University. When I returned on Monday,
I thought, *Oh man, that means the car is going to be stuck
on the other side of Vine Street all day. I need to call her
and propose an alternative.* We allotted only fifteen minutes for rides (thirty minutes round trip), and with all the
congestion on North Broad due to commencement, the
Calhouns would surely hog the car all morning.

There were two choices: Confront Mrs. Calhoun and
cancel her ride, or let it go as scheduled knowing that her
family would likely monopolize the car. I emailed Mrs.
Calhoun to apologize, citing policy and offering to arrange
for private transportation (with a fee). Livid, she called me

immediately to tell me that she felt my decision was a personal attack.

"Has anyone else reserved the car to go to Temple University?" she asked. "Has anyone else reserved the car, period?"

"No. But unfortunately, Mrs. Calhoun, we've taken the car out of service to North Broad Street that day. The car will remain in Center City."

Immediately I called my current manager, Ray, as I knew Mrs. Calhoun would seek him out. And she did, like a cyclone, and gave me an icy glare on the way into his office. Two minutes later, after Mrs. Calhoun exited and walked by swiftly with no eye contact, Ray called me into his office.

"Did you consider how the cancellation would make Mrs. Calhoun feel?" he asked.

Immediately it hit me—I had made the wrong judgment call. "No. I was just following policy."

"Although you did make the wrong choice, I had your back today."

I felt bad that my decision had made someone so incredibly upset. But at the time, I felt like my job was to make decisions that were in the best interest of all residents. And I was grateful Ray validated my authority. Although Ray had stood firm and had my back, I learned rules are meant to be broken for special occasions, and this was a missed opportunity to do something memorable for the Calhouns. We could have filled that car with Temple University swag, balloons, and champagne. My response to Mrs. Calhoun was black and white, and she never looked me in the eyes again.

I now understood that the fair thing isn't always the right thing. At the end of the day, my job was to create memorable moments that brought joy. Hospitality is gray, and sometimes creating a smile takes precedence over the rule.

RUBY

Matchmaker Kathy and her husband, Andy, owned a cat named Ruby, whom they considered their third family member. They traveled a few times a year to their time-share in Mexico and asked me if I wouldn't mind feeding Ruby and scooping poop. I said yes on two conditions: I wouldn't accept payment, and I would be able to be away from my desk for only about five minutes. I had created our original pet policies, which included how and when a staff member could accept employment from a resident, and technically this was off limits. But as a concierge, it was second nature to want to help, and many residents considered their beloved furry friends as important members of the family.

While Kathy and Andy were away, they opted to have some cosmetic work done on their three-bedroom condo and gave me permission to let workers in. This was one of the advantages of condo living, as permission could be left with us to issue a set of house keys to a visitor on the resident's behalf.

On the first day, a sweet orange tabby came frolicking

down the long bedroom corridor. "Hi, Ruby!" I said and petted her on the head. I refilled her bowl, scooped poop, told her, "I'll be back tomorrow," and reminded her to stay out of the workmen's way.

On the second day, Ruby was nowhere to be found, and the workmen had also finished for the day. I scoured the 2,300-square-foot unit, calling out for Ruby, and finally heard a faint meowing. But still no Ruby. The meowing grew louder, and I stood in the living room, perplexed. I finally pressed my ear to a nearby wall, which had been patched and covered over with drywall for the last twenty-four hours, and the meowing grew louder! *No way! Was Ruby in the wall?* I stood there, paralyzed. I certainly wasn't about to bust through Kathy and Andy's freshly painted wall. But I had to do something.

I ran back to the concierge desk and radioed the building engineer. If my suspicions about Ruby's whereabouts were true, I needed someone to knock a hole in the wall immediately! It was the weekend, and I knew Kathy's hired paint crew wasn't returning until Monday. I planned to reach out to Kathy and Andy only once I had a happy, safe, and sound Ruby in my hands. I figured some levity would help the situation as I explained the reopening of the wall and the setback in finishing their living-room project.

Within fifteen minutes, I stood wide-eyed as the workmen sledgehammered and hand sawed to open the living-room wall. I worried they might nick her. The hole was purposely cut around waist height, as they didn't want to cut too close to the ground, where Ruby might be huddled. This meant I had to lean over a gaping hole and attempt to scoop up a terrified cat. Fortunately Ruby's hunger worked in my favor, and she hopped into my arms, purring and completely unscathed.

That had been the last time I volunteered my cat sitting services. I'd also learned that I could engage in difficult conversations with residents. It was okay to share less-than-desirable news as long as I expressed compassion. Ruby's safety had been most important. And I'd also learned that sometimes a short time away from the concierge desk could become a much bigger and longer ordeal.

FISHBOWL

"Who is the young blond?" asked Raazi, head of maintenance, referring to Mr. Kirk's new houseguest.

"How old do you think she is?" asked Lawrence, the morning doorman.

Two Liberty was a fishbowl. Residents' dating lives left us shaking our heads and discussing details in the break room over burritos. If someone is seeking privacy and anonymity, a condo association with a communal lobby and mail room is the last place for them.

So naturally when Mr. Kirk, who was in his mid-sixties, decided to invite a young woman in her early twenties to live with him, the staff and neighbors began to talk. Was she his daughter? No. His only daughter was a few years older and was married with kids. Was she his niece? Nope.

Mr. Kirk, a divorcé, was bald with a neatly trimmed beard. While he was short in stature, his custom sneaker collection made him noticeable the moment he entered a room. In addition, Mr. Kirk was a confirmed bachelor and owner of a prestigious Philadelphia engineering firm.

Until one day a young woman appeared by his side in the lobby.

He never introduced her to us by any title. Only as Brenda. She never came to the thirty-seventh floor to work out or collect mail, so for a while she was just "Who is this woman?" to the concierge staff. I finally heard her voice the day she called me to request the house car. A week later I learned through the staff and security cameras that Brenda had an olive complexion and short curly hair and was working toward a degree in nursing at the local community college. After Brenda moved into Mr. Kirk's giant condo with nothing but a duffel bag, she began to routinely request the house car to transport herself to class, and sometimes Mr. Kirk would call down to schedule the car on her behalf.

Residential concierges become protective of residents, so I wanted to make sure Mr. Kirk was not being taken advantage of. But as a women's studies minor in college, I was feeling protective of Brenda as well. Fortunately, Mr. Kirk had a full-time butler named Bernard who wasn't so tight lipped about the matter.

"Let's just say the guest room isn't being used," he said when I engaged him about the new occupant.

Mr. Kirk's lack of disclosure was just one example of the power divide between affluent residents and staff members. We were there to keep our heads down and not have an opinion on anyone or anything, except as it related to a concierge request. But a yes-sir, no-sir mentality wasn't really the culture of our community except with Mr. Kirk. Mr. Kirk owned a BMW, seven motorcycles, a hand-painted mural of Paris in his den, and a rare collection of Macallan scotch. Brenda, in her new Moncler down jacket, was always on his arm.

A SORT OF PARENT

Keeping our residents safe was a top responsibility of mine. The employee manual instructed us to be the eyes and ears for resident safety, but not the hero. Staff should never touch a resident or get in a confrontational situation. If we were afraid for our safety or a resident's safety, we dialed 911.

I thought of the residents as my children. When they stepped foot into a residential common area, such as the lobby or the club floor, they were under my watch. The goal was to walk a resident to the elevator and make sure the button for the correct floor was pushed, provide an escort, or carefully see that they made it home okay, through the lens of cameras located in every common space. I often wondered if the residents knew how responsible we felt for their well-being.

Alcohol and weed consumption were par for the course with residents, especially on the weekends. Overnight staff members witnessed a wide spectrum of activity, including Tony staggering home from a club at 3:00 a.m. with a young lady friend in ripped jeans. The behavioral patterns were like clockwork.

Until late one night, a young female resident with fluffy blond hair came home after a night out at the bars, drunk, and got off on the club floor on thirty-seven rather than her own floor. After 11:00 p.m., the club floor isn't staffed, and she went to the women's locker room undetected, fell, hit her head, passed out on the floor, and remained there for hours. At some point she came to and shuffled home, again undetected. Although our cameras had the ability to capture her entire journey (except inside the locker room, for privacy reasons), our staff had not paid full attention and had not noticed she was still on the club floor. No one had followed her home with their eyes.

Twenty-four hours later the same resident, with a head injury, sheepishly stopped by the concierge desk to discuss the incident and to see if I could identify how long she had been unconscious. I was able to successfully produce a time stamp and playback of her entering and exiting the locker room. She apologized profusely for the accident—and for the embarrassing task of having to scroll through the video footage of her blunder. I said what I was trained to say: "It was our job to get you safely home, and we dropped the ball."

However, I really thought, *Here is a woman my same age whom I'm having to babysit.*

I'll never know why she got off on the thirty-seventh floor, but we should have been able to react accordingly, and we hadn't. When I shared the story with the overnight team who had worked the shift, they were horrified and vowed to not say anything to the resident, or to others, to respect her privacy. It had taken a misstep to prompt staff to be more vigilant.

Reviewing camera footage to document staff infractions, such as sleeping on the job, was to be expected. But never did I think I'd be reviewing footage on behalf of residents to help keep them safe. Doormen are widely considered to be fancy security guards. But babysitters too? I guess we needed to add that title to their job description. From then on, my mantra was this: "Follow them with your eyes. They are your responsibility until they are in their home."

TUG OF CHANGE

I regularly brought people together for Quizzo trivia, salsa lessons, museum tours, art gallery openings, and food tastings, such as Pennsylvania-themed beer and pretzels.

But one day my favorite resident, Susan, dressed in athleisure, reading glasses, and a smile (I envied her upbeat spirit, tennis playing, and volunteering), walked up to the concierge desk and said, "Jamie, we need a book club. Can you gauge resident interest and set up an introductory meeting?"

"That's a wonderful idea. Why didn't I think of that?"

I had thought of it but was so happy she'd beat me to it with the suggestion.

Susan also asked if I'd be the master of ceremonies at the book club.

"Yes!" I said. "Absolutely!" I loved to read, and since my job description encouraged community building, this type of gathering was a perfect fit. I was excited to bring people together.

Our first meeting took place steps from my desk, in the media room. I showed up right after work, in my charcoal gray uniform, with *Peace Like a River*, by Leif Enger, a novel about a boy in search of an outlawed brother—a book I struggled to read and a protagonist and plot I struggled to identify with. However, because I'd finished the book, I wasn't nervous. As if I were a teacher, I faced the ladies and read from the discussion questions posed by the author. I desperately wanted them to enjoy the evening and their time spent together and to return for a second meeting.

What I didn't anticipate was that a discussion of plot organically turned into personal chitchat: where they had gone to dinner, visits with grandkids, vacation planning.

"I loved the edamame dumplings at Buddakan," I chimed in. "And I am headed to the orchestra next weekend too."

At the book club, I also loved hanging out with Marsha (a retired radiologist), Beverly (an antiques dealer), Barbara (a homemaker), Linda (a real estate agent), and Stacie (a marketing professional) and learning more about them for ninety minutes. Although I was in my twenties and they were mostly in their mid-sixties, I felt like their contemporary. Had I been born in the wrong decade? Maybe. But what I really loved was that each one had had a rich life, and I was able to learn more about them as women and also as wives, mothers, and grandmothers.

After our first meeting and selection of the next date, I assumed I'd hand off the reins to one of the residents to coordinate the next meeting. So it was to my great surprise when Barbara said, "Jamie, we'll see you at the next one?"

I raised my eyebrows. "I would be honored."

When we met again months later, I made sure to go home first, change out of my work clothes, set my DVR to record *Survivor* (my favorite show), and then walk back the ten blocks to work to lead our second meeting.

I floated through the lobby and saw a doorman roll their eyes at the sight of me in street clothes with a book tucked under my arm. I usually worked only from 7:00 a.m. to 3:00 p.m.

"I'm here to facilitate book club," I said, to make sure I wouldn't get in trouble and so the staff knew I was working.

I fobbed myself up to the fortieth floor and knocked on Marsha's door, ready with book club discussion questions for *The Friday Night Knitting Club*, by Kate Jacobs, a book I adored, about women bonding over their shared stories and unexpected sisterhood.

Usually when working, I'd arrive at a resident's threshold to deliver a package, conduct an estimate, or let in a vendor. This time I was welcomed in, asked to take off my shoes, given a glass of wine, and provided a quick tour of Marsha's custom Isaiah Zagar mosaic in the den. Seeing it felt like witnessing a Renoir in person. I was mesmerized by the whimsy and playful mirror-and-tile work covering the wall. When I joined the other ladies, this time on the living-room sofa, they said, "Yay, Jamie's here!" For the first time, I realized I was an invited guest.

As we talked about *Friday Night Knitting*, I saw how we all had fun talking about the characters. Being in Marsha's home made it special. Would we become our own sisterhood? I missed my old coworkers and our camaraderie, the softball team and going to bars straight from work. Now I had none of that, and this book club was the closest thing I'd found since.

Like a character in the book, I began to notice the two worlds I occupied. I felt equally comfortable on Marsha's settee as I did behind the concierge desk. Book club was a place and time to reflect, to listen to other women's intellect, to laugh and have friendly debates (thank you, Beverly!). Occasionally the book club women asked questions about staff members, residents, or new policies, and I made sure to disclose only what Ray, our community manager, would have said if the resident had posed the same question in his office. Except for fielding the occasional attempt to glean community gossip, I never felt like I was the concierge. I felt like I was their younger contemporary, leading them in discussion. I found it easy to socialize. I loved hearing all their perspectives on mental illness, World War II, foot binding in China, and more. As the years passed, the book club ladies and I read fifty-five books. Our time together also included my three years of dating and then getting engaged to the doctor Kathy had set me up with.

In January 2013 Linda suggested our next meeting be held at a restaurant. When I arrived at our table, I looked around and saw everyone holding gifts, not books.

"Surprise!" the ladies said in unison. "Happy engagement!"

The only agenda was wining and dining. We never discussed a book. We ordered and sipped prosecco, and although I was aware that I still worked as their concierge, I was incredibly happy to be surrounded by such thoughtful and generous women.

The next morning, while putting on my uniform and positioning my name tag, I was reminded I was still an employee—and that the book club ladies and their condo fees paid my salary. But I was crossing over from *friendly* to *friend*, and this kind of thing was a no-no in the employee handbook.

At the same time, I felt isolated at work. I found myself unable to relate to Ezedine, our doorman from Addis Ababa, Ethiopia, and Kalilou, from Nigeria, both of whom worked multiple jobs to send money back to their home countries. Nor could I relate to one of my favorite doormen, Dave, who was a recovering addict and had spent time in and out of different treatment facilities. I felt guilty, and I was aware that my coworkers didn't have the same luxury of savings and education. Should I tell them I'd spent the weekend reading a book with my feet in the sand, knowing they'd worked back-to-back shifts?

Because the concierge desk was located on the thirty-seventh floor, I often felt as if I were up on a pedestal when I called on the phone or walkie-talkie to communicate with the lobby staff, to request a resident's car to be brought around or a bell cart be sent up to a unit, or to schedule the house car for a ride. I felt guilty about my demands, but it was all business. I was nervous to misspeak or sound disrespectful, which distanced me even further. If I acted too chummy, it made it impossible when the time came to counsel them. As a result, I withdrew. I stopped trying to build rapport. There was no camaraderie.

And especially since my engagement. All my conversations were about jetting to Budapest with my fiancé for a medical conference; dining at Zahav, rated one of the best restaurants in Philly; and planning a black-tie wedding. I was conflicted but couldn't help the fact that I now had more in common with our residents. I felt the tug of change.

The torn, isolated feeling came to a head one afternoon during a routine staff meeting in the sun-drenched boardroom on the fifty-seventh floor, a penthouse that later sold for just shy of $11 million. I sat opposite Dwayne, our morning driver, who was in his early twenties and aspired to become a firefighter.

"You're a bitch," he calmly told me in front of the entire team. "You're condescending, you're judgmental, you micromanage us—"

I pivoted in my swivel seat, wanting to defend myself. But was it my place to do so? I wanted someone else to speak up and come to my defense, but the silence continued. I couldn't find my voice to fight back. I sat stunned, looking past Dwayne's silhouette to the westerly views and sky, unable to speak. I thought about leaving. But if I left the room, I would admit defeat. Instead, I decided to be stoic, letting the rage boil up inside but not allowing tears to form. I didn't want to let the rest of the team know how much his words had hurt me.

Nobody, not even Ray, our community manager, came to my defense. Was there truth in what Dwayne had said? Ray eventually made a segue, but he never addressed the accusation. Although it was never mentioned again, Dwayne had crossed a line that day. His actions were intentional, staged to hurt and humiliate me in front of a dozen colleagues.

Given there was no recourse and no follow-up mediation, the next day at work was business as usual. I called Dwayne numerous times to tell him I'd scheduled the house car to transport a resident, and he politely answered and did as I'd asked. There was no hiding away in a cubicle. I had no choice but to communicate with him throughout my shift, even though I was still reeling from the accusation the day before.

That weekend, while strolling Rittenhouse Square, I

pondered how we know when it is the right time to leave a job. The incident in the boardroom was a clear sign. After seven years of creating community and fostering relationships, I was no longer feeling fulfilled by my day job. The concierge position used to feel glamorous, but not anymore. Where I had once felt proud of my work, now I questioned it. *What am I still doing here?* But I wasn't going to run away. I wanted to leave to do something bigger. Bolder. I needed an exit strategy. And this time I knew Craigslist wouldn't have the answer.

DEPARTURE

OVER THE RAINBOW

When the management contract at the Residences at Two Liberty Place wasn't renewed in 2014, it was the perfect time for me to walk away. Alexa and Sharon were going to stay on under the new management company, and the concierge desk was in great hands. My marriage, and the safety net of a second income, gave me the cushion to start my own business. This was the window of opportunity I had been looking for.

I loved being an adjunct professor, teaching an introduction to hospitality class each semester, which I'd started doing as soon as I had earned my master's from Temple. But I knew I didn't want to teach full-time. Instead I wanted to train customer-facing employees to make fabulous first impressions, paying homage to the foundational training I'd received at the Rittenhouse. I wanted to train them how to provide personalized service and anticipate the needs of their customers from the point of view of a concierge.

And where would I get my content for trainings?

From moments of truth over the last decade.

Each customer interaction I had, whether positive, negative, or neutral, resulted in its own story and lesson.

POST-STAY

TEN YEARS LATER

At the Ritz-Carlton in Sarasota, Florida, I find my way to the ballroom, where I will be a keynote speaker for a travel company's semiannual educational summit. After the tech guy fished a wire up my blouse and handed me a microphone, I realize I have to pee, and I take it all apart.

Back on stage, a hundred audience members applaud as I'm introduced.

"Good morning!" I roar. "I'm excited to share with you today the 'Five Keys to Service Excellence' that made the biggest impact on the customer during my decade-long career as a concierge."

And I confidently share these keys:

- Give personalized attention
- Anticipate needs
- Underpromise, overdeliver
- Take ownership
- Provide timely service recovery; make the person forget why they're upset in the first place

At the end, I ask the audience to pick one thing to focus on in their effort to reach higher to serve the customer. Because I know the smallest of self-aware details can make a huge impact.

After a round of applause, I exit the ballroom, starving (I can never eat before a morning keynote), and I think of traveling home to my husband and daughter.

At the Ritz's concierge desk, I ask for help printing my boarding pass, a task I performed hundreds of times at the Rittenhouse. I still prefer the real deal in my hand! Brylee, a young woman in her early twenties wearing a crisp white blouse, a scarf that matched her brown hair, and a name tag, greets me with a smile.

Once she asks for my name to pull up the reservation, she realizes who I am because she'd booked my car service from the airport.

"Oh, Ms. Cooperstein!" she says. "It's a pleasure to meet you in person!"

"So nice to meet you. Did you know I used to be a concierge? It changed my life."

Brylee tells me she's been a concierge for only six weeks. Long enough to be hooked. It is her first full-time job out of college.

"Really!" I say, and I chuckle, feeling like I'm looking in a mirror reflecting a different period of my life. And for a moment, everything points back to the uniformed girl at the podium in the lobby of the Rittenhouse. I would love to be in her shoes, serving the guest again. I miss standing in a hotel lobby, securing a tough dinner reservation on a Saturday night for a guest that has just checked in. I miss building a full-day itinerary of the Brandywine Valley. I miss surprising someone on their anniversary with an in-room amenity of chocolate-covered strawberries and champagne.

Brylee hands me my boarding pass. "Your driver is here."

I thank her and hand her a crisp twenty-dollar bill and my business card.

Although I no longer have the title of concierge, the pride and passion to serve others that came from that job will forever ooze through my veins. The concierge role transformed me and my interpersonal relationships with others. Today, when I'm coaching individuals on the importance of making a fabulous first impression, I think back fondly on this period of my life, where I, too, wore a uniform, smiled so much it hurt, and, on a good day, made a lot of other people smile as well.

I wanted to tell Brylee all the things I'd learned about true hospitality and how I grew over that ten-year span.

But that was my story. Her story is just beginning.

ACKNOWLEDGMENTS

Thank you for making it this far!

The writing of this book required me to tap into my personal and professional Rolodex, a must-have for any concierge. And it is *only* because of my network, my team, that my book has reached you.

I'd first like to thank the people who inspired this book.

Mom: Because of your suggestion to call Cousin Jeffrey, I stepped into the magical world of hospitality and found my calling. Moms really do know best. I love you!

Dad: I had to fake it for a long time but once I made it as a concierge, I never looked back. Thanks for always having my back!

Jeff Berger: You got me my interview at the Rittenhouse. The rest, they say, is history. I am eternally grateful.

Lucia Pernot: Thank you for taking a chance on a twenty-two-year-old girl from Delco who had endless ambition and no industry experience.

David Benton: Although you made me nervous back then (and still do), you inspired me and pushed me to see that wearing a uniform was a great privilege. I still challenge myself to find new ways to wow customers because of the foundation you laid.

Frank Marandino: I wouldn't have lasted beyond my ninety-day introductory period without your belief in me and seeing you effortlessly model "true hospitality."

Richard Oller: You have been such a cheerleader and supporter from the very first day we met atop Two Liberty Place. It was your vision of white-glove lifestyle services that I helped to execute for the lucky people who called Two Liberty Place home. I hope this book continues to make you proud.

Alex Cohen, Kimberly Horvath, and Ray Kennedy: While your leadership styles as general manager and community manager at Two Liberty varied widely, I learned a great deal from each of you and was able to hone my own style as a result.

And now for the people that helped me cross the finish line to become an author!

Jennifer Schelter: My writing coach and accountability partner. I never realized how hard it was to write a book and how brutal the revision process could be. You held my hand every step of the way. When I wanted to quit, you believed in me and my book and pushed me to make it something I'm immensely proud of. You also somehow pulled memories from me that I didn't even know I still held. I can't wait for the opportunity to work together again!

Anne Dubuisson: Your review of my manuscript and insights into the vast world of publishing gave me direction and, most importantly, led me to the team at Girl Friday Productions.

Jordyn Robinson: When we started working together years ago, I never knew how much you loved books, especially paperbacks. Thank you for the many, many things you've helped with along the way to make sure readers love my book as well.

Fran Nachman: My dear concierge friend, you were my earliest reader, and my book is better because of your suggestions.

Jordana Ostroff: Thank you for always asking how my book was coming along, which motivated me to always have a new update to share with you.

The Girl Friday team: When I was shopping for publishers, I dreamed of having my own publishing concierge. Kim Kent, you have been my personal Five Diamond concierge and more. And Matthew Patin—wow, you are a gifted editor. My book has been elevated beyond my wildest dreams because of your keen eye and thought-provoking analysis. Karen Upson, Adria Batt, and everyone else—thank you for believing in my story and supporting me to stay on schedule and get this book into the hands of my target readers.

And last, but not least . . .

Josh and Josephine: You're my why. You loved me unconditionally, even when I was stressed, up against a tight deadline, or had a headache from staring at my manuscript for too long. You have been my cheerleaders since day one. We can do hard things, and I love you both so much!

And finally, thank *you* for reading my book! Whether you wanted an insider look at the world of luxury hospitality or simply wanted to reminisce or commiserate with the many demands and privileges of a unique career, I hope you found what you were looking for!

DISCUSSION GUIDE

Facilitating book club discussions is something I love to do! So I wanted to make it as easy as possible for readers to continue the dialogue about some of the themes and lessons I've unpacked in *True Hospitality*. While these discussion prompts were predominantly written for someone who currently, formerly, or hopes to work in hospitality, anyone can benefit from them. Just answer based on how you would handle the situation or apply it to your current or former profession.

I also encourage you to please reach out at info@ jcoopconsulting.com if you'd like for me to drop by your book club.

1. While at her senior internship at Fox 29, an interaction completely changed Jamie's outlook on her future. Have you faced a similar roadblock? If so, how did you respond?

2. Jamie's cousin Jeff opened up a door for her to begin a career in luxury hospitality. Who in your network has opened up a door for you? Have you been successful in opening up a door for someone else?

3. Jamie was a fish out of water during her first few months on the job, yet she was forced to hide her insecurities and radiate confidence. When was a time you had to overcome vulnerabilities in the workplace?

4. Frank is an effortless concierge who taught Jamie a lot about what she knows. Who in your life has mentored you in a similar way?

5. Throughout *True Hospitality*, there are many memorable customer interactions at both the Rittenhouse and Two Liberty. If you are a customer-facing employee, share a time you wowed a customer. Or if you are usually the customer, when was a time you were on the receiving end of great service?

6. Jamie categorized three types of hotel employees—the Hotel Lifer, Hotel Climber, and Résumé Filler. Do you relate to this categorization when it comes to a career in hospitality? And if so, which one are you?

7. Even though her manager had her back, Jamie regrets a decision she made that negatively affected a resident and their family. When was a time you made a wrong judgment call, and how did it make you feel? Did your manager support you?

8. An unfortunate incident took place at a work staff meeting that blindsided Jamie and left her reeling. Have you ever had a confrontation in the workplace? If so, how did you respond?

9. Some may find certain customer requests to be shocking or surprising, like a young bride wanting a Botox appointment in the days leading up to her wedding. How have you removed bias or prejudice in a situation that was at odds with your own personal beliefs?

10. A pivotal moment in Jamie's career was when she had to work on Super Bowl Sunday when her hometown Philadelphia Eagles were playing. Was there a time you had to miss a special event for work purposes? If so, how did you handle that disappointment or frustration?

11. Hospitality is often a gray area, and Jamie frequently had to make on-the-spot decisions, like scheduling the Rittenhouse's house car. Share a time when you had to make a difficult decision and went against policy for a guest's happiness.

12. Have you ever helped a celebrity while on the job? If so, how did you handle the encounter? Were they similar to or different from what you were expecting?

13. What is your favorite hotel you've ever stayed in, and why?

14. Jamie outlines many of the positives and negatives of being a concierge. Is it a job or career path you'd ever consider or recommend to others? Why or why not?

ABOUT THE AUTHOR

© Sammi Shea

Jamie Cooperstein teaches companies, employees, and students to enhance the customer experience—a natural extension of her decade spent as a Five Diamond concierge. As a speaker and trainer, she infuses both storytelling and interactive exercises into her programs to make sure that attendees leave both feeling motivated and with the necessary tools for reinforcement. As a consultant, she helps bridge gaps between managers and those working in the trenches for the benefit of the customers.

Prior to opening J. Cooperstein Hospitality Consulting,

LLC, a certified Women Business Enterprise (WBE), Jamie spent ten years in uniform, most notably as a concierge at the AAA Five Diamond–designated Rittenhouse Hotel and Condominiums in Philadelphia.

She is a former president of the Philadelphia Area Concierge Association and has obtained her master's degree in tourism and hospitality management from Temple University. Jamie lives in the Society Hill section of Philadelphia with her husband and daughter.

LET'S CONNECT:

info@jcoopconsulting.com
@jcoopconsulting
www.jcoopconsulting.com